American REBELS

James Dean

"Dream As If You'll Live Forever"

Karen Clemens Warrick

Enslow Publishers, Inc.
40 Industrial Road
Box 398
Berkeley Heights, NJ 07922
USA
http://www.enslow.com

Library of Congress Cataloging-in-Publication Data

Warrick, Karen Clemens.
James Dean : "dream as if you'll live forever" / Karen Clemens Warrick.
p. cm. — (American rebels)
Includes bibliographical references and index.
ISBN 0-7660-2537-3
1. Dean, James, 1931–1955—Juvenile literature. 2. Motion picture actors and actresses—United States—Biography—Juvenile literature. I. Title. II. Series.
PN2287.D33W37 2006
791.4302'8092—dc22
[B]
2006005893

Printed in the United States of America

10 9 8 7 6 5 4 3 2 1

To Our Readers: We have done our best to make sure all Internet Addresses in this book were active and appropriate when we went to press. However, the author and the publisher have no control over and assume no liability for the material available on those Internet sites or on other Web sites they may link to. Any comments or suggestions can be sent by e-mail to comments@enslow.com or to the address on the back cover.

Illustration Credits: Associated Press/AP, p. 15; Classmates Media, Inc., p. 41; TM/©2006 James Dean, Inc. by CMG Worldwide, Inc., www.JamesDean.com, pp. 7, 9, 24, 55, 66, 76, 86, 99, 111, 120; Library of Congress, p. 93.

Cover Illustration: TM/©2006 James Dean, Inc. by CMG Worldwide, Inc., www.JamesDean.com.

Contents

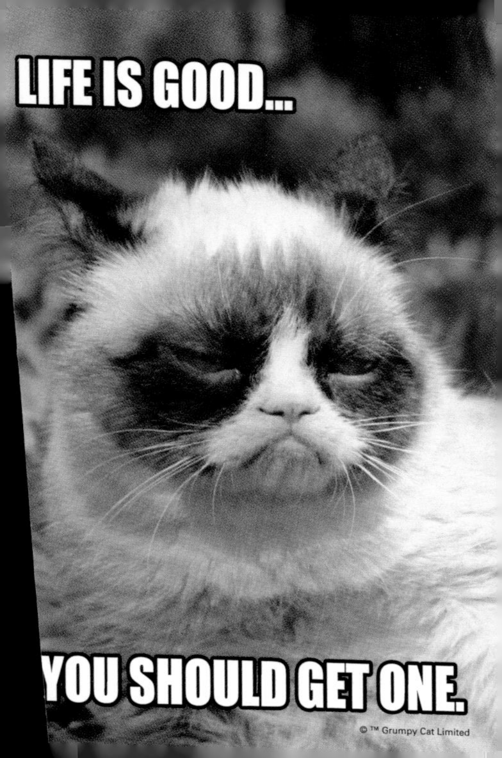

LIFE IS GOOD...

YOU SHOULD GET ONE.

GCS1Bulk series
sticker 2 of 10

Grumpy Cat®

SandyLion
Published and distributed by
Trends International LLC, Indianapolis, IN 46268 USA
www.trendsinternational.com

Made in the USA
TRUS10000014592
02172015

Chapter 1

The Big Break

On April 8, 1954, James Dean walked out of his New York apartment carrying two paper bags stuffed with clothes tied together with kitchen string. A limousine waited at the curb with Director Elia Kazan inside. The two of them were flying to Hollywood. Kazan was about to begin filming his newest blockbuster production, *East of Eden*. Dean, an unknown actor, was to play one of the leading characters.

The twenty-three-year-old tried to portray a tough, cool character as he boarded the plane, but his act was unconvincing. He looked more like a nervous child to Kazan.[1] For most of the flight, he sat with his nose pressed against the window. It was his first airplane ride.

Dean had been to California before. In fact, he had lived in Los Angeles as a child with his mother and father for four years. His father, Winton Dean, still lived in the area. After landing, the young actor asked to stop by the hospital where his father worked. The reunion was short, and Winton Dean showed no affection toward his son. Kazan remembered "a strong tension between the two and it was not friendly. I sensed the father disliked his son. [He] didn't seem to think his son's future very promising. They stood side by side, but talk soon collapsed, and we drove on."[2]

This brief meeting helped Kazan determine the focus for his movie plot based on John Steinbeck's novel, *East of Eden*. It is the story of a son trying to please his disapproving father, a contemporary version of the biblical tale of Cain and Abel. Dean's character, Caleb Trask tries desperately to win his father's approval and love, but his brother Aron is the one to earn their father's praise. In the end though, Aron gets drunk and goes off to war, disappointing his father. It is Cal who stands by Adam Trask, caring for him after he is paralyzed by a stroke.

The director decided the script must spotlight the bitter relationship between Adam Trask and his son Caleb. It needed to mirror Dean's relationship with his own father. "Jimmy . . . *was* Cal," Kazan said. . . . "He had a grudge against fathers. He was vengeful, he had a sense of aloneness and of being persecuted, and he was suspicious." Kazan felt certain that he had hired the right actor for the role of Cal.[3] Dean's personal experiences would create a powerful emotional impact in the movie.

Hollywood Scene

Rehearsals would begin in two weeks. Kazan wanted Dean to gain ten pounds and get a suntan before then. He ordered him to go to the desert. Dean did not want

Before he left for California, James Dean had Roy Schatt take this picture of him in front of an apartment-rental sign.

to go alone, so he invited his old college roommate, Bill Bast, along. They rented a Ford convertible and drove to Borrego Springs, California, to soak up some rays.

After a week, the two returned to the city. Dean had an appointment with agent Dick Clayton to review the contract Warner Bros. had offered him. For his first movie, he would earn about one thousand dollars a week. It was a standard contract. Even though he had a starring role in *East of Eden*, James Dean was an unknown.

Publicity was important in the movie industry, especially for a newcomer like Dean. The studio arranged for Hollywood gossip columnist Hedda Hopper to interview him. The young actor gave his best "spoiled brat" performance. He slouched in his seat in the studio cafeteria, refused to say anything, then spit at a portrait of one of the movie stars hanging on the wall. Hopper was unimpressed. She dismissed Dean as a "dirty-shirt-tailed boy in blue jeans."[4]

Before filming began, Dean and Bast bumped into Paul Newman, another young actor. The last time Dean saw Newman was in New York when they both auditioned for the parts in *East of Eden*.

"You're a lucky devil," Newman said. "I wanted that part in *Eden* so bad I could taste it. . . . It's a rough business. If you're lucky, you can make it . . . like you, Jim. If you don't get the breaks, I mean. . . . You just can't get there on your own hook."

"Nuts!" Dean said, "That's not true!"

"Come off it, Dean," Newman said. "You can't tell me no one helped you . . . made things a little easier for you."

This famous photo of James Dean walking in New York City was taken by Roy Schatt in 1954.

"No one ever did anything for me," Dean shouted. "I did it myself. I don't owe anything to anyone! Not one stinking penny." To emphasize his point, Dean pounded his fist on the table. He trembled, he was so angry. Newman changed the subject, ending the argument.[5] It was clear that James Dean did not want to be indebted to anyone.

It was clear that James Dean did not want to be indebted to anyone.

In fact, Dean had worked for this moment since the time he was a child in Indiana, playacting with his mother and performing in school dramas. These positive experiences encouraged him to pursue an acting career, to reach for the stars. His dream was now within reach, and twenty-three-year-old James Byron Dean was prepared to hold on with a death grip.

Chapter 2

James Byron Dean

James Byron Dean was born on February 8, 1931, in Marion, Indiana, about seventy miles north of Indianapolis. He was the only child of Winton and Mildred Wilson Dean.

Winton Dean grew up on a farm near Fairmount, eleven miles south of Marion. He did not like farming and trained to be a dental technician. In 1930, he got a job at the Veterans Administration in Marion. Winton was a tall, handsome young man. He worked hard, but had little curiosity about the rest of the world. He was quite satisfied staying in the community where he had been born and raised.

Mildred Wilson grew up on a farm near Gas City, Indiana, a few miles north of Fairmount. She loved to learn, had a keen sense of humor, and was interested in art, music, and poetry. She dreamed of traveling abroad.[1]

Her mother, Minnie, died of cancer a few months

after Mildred graduated from high school. She had loved her mother dearly and was paralyzed by grief. For weeks she did nothing but sit at home and cry. When her father remarried less than a year later, Mildred packed and moved to Marion. She found a clerical job, met Winton Dean, and one month later, she was pregnant.

A Wedding

Winton and Mildred had dated for only a few weeks. They had little in common, but in the 1930s, it was scandalous to have a baby and not be married. So on July 26, 1930, they wed. The groom was twenty-two, the bride nineteen. Years later, the date on the Deans' marriage certificate was changed to 1929. The earlier wedding date made the birth of their baby more acceptable.[2]

The young couple rented rooms at a boardinghouse. Winton filled his days with work at the Veterans Administration Hospital. He felt lucky to have a good position, since the country was in the middle of the Great Depression, a ten-year period when banks failed, unemployment was high, and the stock market crashed.[3]

Mildred Dean spent her days getting ready for the birth of their baby. She redecorated their apartment, painting every room. Whenever possible, she also used money she saved to escape on little adventures. She would board a bus for Indianapolis by herself. In the city, she went to variety shows and dance recitals. Sometimes she attended plays at the Indianapolis Civic Theater.

To fill evenings at home, Mildred tried to entertain her husband by reciting poetry. Indiana poet James Whitcomb Riley was one of her favorites, but Winton showed no interest in her performances.

A Baby Boy

Only six months and thirteen days after Mildred and Winton married, James Byron Dean was born. A myth has grown up over the years about the baby's middle name. Fans claim his mother named him after the famous English poet, Lord Byron. However, no one in the family believes that to be true.[4] He was actually named after two of his father's friends.

Jimmy weighed eight pounds, ten ounces, and the doctor bill for his delivery was fifteen dollars. Mildred doted on her son. She held and cuddled him constantly. Relatives scolded her for spoiling the boy.[5] Winton, a working father, spent much less time with his son. Even from the start, he showed little affection toward Jimmy.[6]

As Jimmy grew up, he seemed to be happy, but his childhood was far from perfect. His mother and father were not well matched. They did not share the same interests. They disagreed on what was best for their son. Also, times were tough in the 1930s. Many Americans were out of work because of the Depression. Banks were failing. Families went without food, clothing, and a roof over their heads. For many, the situation grew desperate. Some turned to a life of crime to survive. When Jimmy was born, Marion ranked eighth among Indiana towns for violent crime.

Two years later, Indiana's infamous criminal John Dillinger was paroled. Within eight months, he robbed a dozen banks in and around the state. Everyone feared their town would be the gangster's next target.

Mother and Son

Even with Winton's steady job, the Dean family struggled to make ends meet. Between 1932 and 1936, they moved four times. The homes were modest, and each time Mildred painted the walls with bright new colors. The baby's birth also ended her trips to Indianapolis for recitals and plays. There was not enough money for those extras. Mildred settled into a new routine. She spent her free time entertaining herself and her captive audience of one.

Jimmy was a bright, healthy baby. He talked early and by age two spoke in complete sentences. At three, his mother gave him crayons and taught him to draw. Jimmy loved this activity. In fact, Mildred had trouble getting him to stop when it was time to do other things, like eat and sleep.

About this time, Jimmy began to have some unusual health problems. He had many nosebleeds and sometimes fainted. Mildred took him to the doctor. The doctor could find nothing wrong. He assured her that Jimmy would outgrow the problem, and he did.

From the time he was born, Mildred sang and played music for Jimmy. As he grew older, she acted out nursery rhymes. She read him books about rowdy characters like Mike Fink, Captain Stormalong, and Davy Crockett.

Dean spent many years of his childhood in this home in Fairmount, Indiana.

She recited poems for him. Mildred wanted her son to grow up appreciating the arts as much as she did.[7]

Jimmy especially enjoyed tall tales from American folklore. When Mildred dramatized the story of Paul Bunyan, he got into the act. He played the roles of Babe the Blue Ox and Johnny Inkslinger. Mildred pretended to be Paul. The front porch of their house served as a stage. Neighbors remember watching the performances of mother and son. They fought off enemies, negotiated rapids, and struggled through blizzards. They pretended to be all kinds of characters from American Indians to raccoons.

Jimmy especially enjoyed tall tales from American folklore.

Mildred told Jimmy the story of Johnny Appleseed. She also shared the true story of John Chapman, the man who inspired the legendary character. Chapman had lived and died in Indiana not far from their home. After hearing the story, Jimmy asked his mother for apple seeds. He wanted to raise an orchard in his backyard. He planted the seeds and acted out the tale of Johnny Appleseed for other children in the neighborhood. Unfortunately, the Deans moved before his trees had time to grow.

Mildred often took Jimmy to movies. After they saw the Disney cartoon, *The Three Little Pigs*, four-year-old Jimmy imitated all the characters. He danced, sang, and blew the house down.

Mildred also played games with her son. For one of their games she built a cardboard theater. They used dolls as actors, and the two of them made up plays and stories. From time to time they put on skits for Winton and other family members. Both Mildred and Jimmy loved to hear the applause when the play was over. Mildred was fond of saying that one day her beautiful son was going to be a great actor.[8]

Father and Son

As Jimmy grew older his relationship with his father did not get any better. He later said, "I never understood what he [Winton] was after, what sort of person he'd been, because he never tried to get on my side of the fence, or to try and see things the way I saw them when I was little. I was always with Mom and we were very close."[9]

Winton remembered how curious Jimmy was about many things. He noted, too, that his son quickly lost interest in them: "He had a large anxiety to do many different things. He had to try everything, and he soon outgrew most of the toys we bought him."[10]

Winton also remembered Jimmy's stubbornness. He found it almost impossible to discipline him. "You'd try to order him to do or not do something and he'd just sit there with his little face all screwed up and closed. It didn't take you very long to realize that you weren't going to get anywhere with him. Spanking didn't help. Scolding didn't. And you couldn't bribe him."[11]

Winton did not approve of his son's acting, even as imaginative child's play. He thought that acting was something done by people who were "a little odd."[12]

That was a belief many shared at the time. He wanted to see Jimmy engaged in more rugged, physical activities. He bought his son a baseball, bat, and catcher's glove for his fifth birthday. That spring, the two of them tossed a ball back and forth. Unfortunately, Jimmy did not seem to have the coordination necessary to catch and throw.

Mildred insisted that Jimmy was not clumsy. She thought he was having trouble seeing the ball. Winton took his son to the Medical Center for an eye exam. Mildred was right. Jimmy was extremely nearsighted. He needed glasses. Soon, with the help of his new glasses, he was catching and tossing a ball without a problem. He even asked Winton for a basketball.

A Sick Little Boy

In the summer of 1936, the active five-year-old grew pale and sickly. Jimmy had little energy. He was always tired and constantly had a low-grade fever. He broke out in a rash. It covered his arms, upper body, and legs. These physical ailments worried his mother. A few days later, the symptoms grew worse. He could keep nothing down and vomited up a sticky black fluid. By now, Mildred was convinced that Jimmy was dying.[13] She feared he had cancer like her mother.

Winton and Mildred took their son to the Veterans Administration Medical Center. After two days of testing, the doctors determined that he had severe anemia. The condition was serious, but treatable. They prescribed blood transfusions and vitamins, the only cure known at the time. Though doctors had figured out what was wrong with Jimmy, they did not know the cause of his illness. Now, it is known that he was exposed to poisons. His condition was a direct result of his mother's habit of painting the rooms of each new house. In the 1930s, ordinary house paints contained large amounts of lead, a poisonous substance. While his mother redecorated, Jimmy inhaled paint fumes laced with the dangerous chemical. It is even possible that he, like many children, picked up paint chips and put them in his mouth.

When Jimmy was released from the hospital, he and his parents moved to the country. Winton rented a cheerful little cottage alongside a creek. It was a few miles from Marion on a farm owned by Ortense and Marcus Winslow, Winton's sister and brother-in-law. Jimmy's aunt helped Mildred nurse him back to health.

A farm was a perfect place for the five-year-old to regain his strength. There were 178 acres to run and play on, and dogs, horses, hogs, and cows to play with. Uncle Marcus rigged up a swing on a tree for Jimmy. When he finished with his chores, Marcus played with him. The two took long walks, went swimming, and fished for minnows.

When Jimmy was strong and healthy again, Mildred signed him up for violin lessons. She also enrolled him in dance classes. The youngster enjoyed tap dancing. He mastered the basics so quickly he performed in a dance recital program that fall. Jimmy's violin and tap lessons did not last long. His father came home from work one night with some important news.

A Move West

The Veterans Administration had offered Winton a job in Los Angeles, California. He would be the director of a dental laboratory. The pay was better, the position more prestigious. Winton had decided to accept. He may have seen this move west as an opportunity to leave his wife and son behind. They did not share a close family relationship. Mildred, however, was thrilled with the idea.[14] She immediately made preparations to leave Indiana and move to sunny California.

That fall, Jimmy's grandparents, Charles and Emma Dean went to the railway station to see Winton, Mildred, and Jimmy off.

Chapter 3

Growing Up in L.A.

The Deans moved into a house in Santa Monica, a suburb of Los Angles in 1936. It was a comfortable bungalow with two bedrooms, a living room, and a grassy front yard. A garden grew in back. The Pacific Ocean was only two miles away. The family adjusted to life in California quickly. They enjoyed the sunny year-round weather, especially after Indiana's cold winters.[1]

Winton drove to work each weekday while Mildred took care of the house and her son. There was always something to do in the large city. She enjoyed the variety of activities available, but did miss her family and friends.[2] Mildred often wrote to the folks in Indiana. The letters included lots of photos of Jimmy. His grandparents treasured these snapshots. It helped them watch Jimmy grow up from a distance. Grandma Dean remembered what a "sweet-looking child" he was. His features reminded her of "a china doll, almost too dainty for a boy" and she said he had the "complexion of a ripe apple."[3]

One snapshot his grandma saved showed Jimmy soon after the move to California. He posed for the camera in front of their new home. The six-year-old was dressed in bib overalls with a straw hat perched on his head. He looked like he still lived on the farm. The only clue that Jimmy was in Los Angeles was a spiky yucca plant pictured in the background.

School Days

Jimmy started school in West Los Angeles. He first attended Brentwood Elementary. Then he transferred to McKinley School in the middle of the year. The school was within walking distance of the Dean home. Students teased Jimmy when he started first grade. They made fun of his Indiana accent and his funny middle name. Apparently, Jimmy did little to defend himself from the teasing. No one remembered him fighting or trying to get even with kids who tormented him. Elementary-school classmates and teachers were interviewed after his death. No one remembered much of anything about James Byron Dean, even though he spent three years at McKinley.[4]

During his early school years, Jimmy looked like a sturdy little boy, but he had several physical ailments. He had frequent nosebleeds. He also had problems with internal bleeding that left black-and-blue marks on this arms and legs.

At the end of each school day, Jimmy went home to

spend time with his mother. They often took the streetcar to the Santa Monica pier and explored the waterfront and beach. They dramatized stories, read poetry, and listened to music together as they had in Indiana.

Once Jimmy could write, his mother encouraged a new activity called the wishing game. Before going to bed each night, Jimmy would write a wish on a piece of paper. He put the note under his pillow. During the night, Mildred would slip in and read the note. If possible, she made her son's wish come true.[5]

Except for the hours he was in school, Mildred and Jimmy were almost always together. He had no time for playmates his own age. The creative activities he and his mother shared enriched his life, but Jimmy did not learn how to get along with his peers. Outings with her son probably helped Mildred take her mind off her marriage.[6] California living had not improved her relationship with Winton.[7] As Jimmy and his mother grew closer, there was little space left for Winton. He became a distant figure in his son's life.[8]

A Tragic Illness

In the fall of 1939, Mildred got sick. The early symptoms, similar to those of a stomach virus, did not clear up. As fall turned to winter, she complained of nausea and terrible lower-back pains. She lost thirty pounds. Finally in early April, Mildred went to the doctor. She was diagnosed with cervical cancer. The disease was already in an advanced stage. The doctor

When James Dean was a boy, his mom tried to grant him his wishes. As an adult, he often granted his child fans their wish by giving them his autograph.

immediately put her in the hospital and removed her reproductive organs.

After she recovered from surgery, Mildred went home, but she continued to deteriorate as the cancer spread. She was often in great pain. Soon Mildred was too weak to get out of bed. To take her mind off her discomfort, she liked listening to passages from the Bible.[9] Jimmy sat in a chair by her bed and read aloud verses Mildred requested or ones that he liked. Often he read the twenty-third psalm. It was his favorite.[10]

Other times, Mildred asked her son to read articles to her from magazines. When his mother closed her eyes and she seemed to be asleep, Jimmy continued reading, but his voice dropped to a soft whisper. "I just knew she was asleep before I got through the story," he recalled. "Then she woke up and said, 'I'm listening, Jimmy, I only had my eyes closed.'"[11]

Every night before bedtime, he slipped into his mother's room to say good night.

Every night before bedtime, he slipped into his mother's room to say good night. Jimmy needed to be sure that she was still alive. He developed his own little test. He touched her eyelids gently with a finger. This seemed to assure him that she was only asleep.[12]

Final Days

"How do you tell an eight-year-old boy his mother's going to die?" Winton Dean later asked a reporter from *Modern Screen* magazine. (Jimmy was actually nine at the time.) "She [Mildred] was only twenty-nine. The doctors told me it was hopeless. I tried [to explain it], but I couldn't. . . . Jim and I—we'd never had that closeness. And my Jim is a tough boy to understand."[13]

Though Winton had trouble explaining Mildred's condition to Jimmy, he did inform the family back in Indiana. He wrote to his mother, Emma Dean, describing his wife's illness. In Fairmount, Emma Dean took her son's letter to her own doctor. He read the symptoms and explained that Mildred most likely had eight weeks to live, maybe less.

Prepared for the worst, Grandma Dean took a train to Los Angles to help the family. She arrived in May and found that cancer had changed her daughter-in-law's appearance dramatically. By early June, the doctors said Mildred had only days to live.

"Jim and I—we'd never had that closeness. And my Jim is a tough boy to understand."

Grandma Emma was a great help. She took care of the house and her grandson. In a letter Emma wrote to the family, she mentioned that Mildred "didn't want to die and leave Jimmy until she could get him raised."[14]

By June, Mildred was back in the hospital. "I tried to get it across to him," said Winton of his conversations with Jimmy, "to prepare him in some way, but he just couldn't seem to take it in. I told him straight out one evening: 'Your mother's never coming home again.' All he did was stare at me. Even as a child he wasn't much to talk about his hurts."[15]

After a few days in the hospital, the doctors decided there was nothing more they could do. They sent Mildred home, and on July 14, 1940, she died at age twenty-nine.

Jimmy was down the street playing with a friend when she passed away. A neighbor remembered the child's reaction when the family broke the news to him. "He took it pretty mature. He didn't get hysterical or anything like that. He was troubled. He was a very alert and intelligent child. He didn't start screaming or crying or anything."[16]

Jimmy kept his feelings locked up inside. He had lost his mother. She was the one who loved him most, who had taken care of him, and filled his free time with activities he'd grown to love. The nine-year-old was overwhelmed by her death.

Gone but Not Forgiven

Jimmy never forgot his mother. For the rest of his life, her memory haunted him, and he never completely recovered from her loss. Eight years later, as a senior in high school, he wrote in a short autobiography: "I never knew the reason for Mom's death, in fact it still preys on my mind."[17]

Some years later, Barbara Glenn, an actress Dean dated, said that the two of them "talked about his mother a great deal when we first met. I don't know that it wasn't a resemblance to her that attracted Jimmy to me. He told me I looked like her."[18]

When she asked him what his mother was like,

Jimmy told Glenn that Mildred "had long black hair, that she was thin and very beautiful. He said that she was soft and very gentle and he felt very loved by her."[19]

Glenn also remembered:

> [Dean's] terrible anger for his mother. She died [and left him alone]. When he talked about her it wasn't as a twenty-one or twenty-two-year-old. It was a child and he [felt] deserted. He'd loved her desperately. I think it [his mother's death] had a profound effect on him.[20]

No Mother or Father

After Mildred's death, Winton faced the problems of a single father with no family living nearby to help care for his son. Grandma Dean suggested Jimmy go back to Fairmount. Aunt Ortense and Uncle Marcus had offered to take care of him. When Winton heard the idea, he thought about it for a few minutes then decided that Jimmy would be better off with his family in Indiana. He respected his brother-in-law and knew his sister would "mother" Jimmy better than any housekeeper he could hire. His decision was made. His son would go back to Fairmount to live with his aunt, uncle, and cousin.

After a funeral service in Santa Monica, Mildred's body was shipped by rail to Indiana. Jimmy and Grandma Dean traveled on the same train, called the *Challenger*. It was a trip the youngster would never forget. At every stop, he jumped out and ran to the baggage compartment. He was afraid that someone might remove his mother's coffin before they arrived in Indiana.[21]

Dean later recalled his feelings about this trip back to Indiana. "It seemed to me worse than dying itself."[22] Though the trip was something of a nightmare for the nine-year-old, he asked the conductor for a souvenir. The conductor gave him a cup and saucer with the *Challenger*'s monogram. He kept them always.

Mildred's coffin rested in the Winslows' living room in Fairmount for two days. Relatives remember Jimmy's last moments with his mother. He walked to the coffin for a final look. He straightened out her bangs, and then snipped off a lock of her hair as a keepsake.

He straightened out her bangs, and then snipped off a lock of her hair as a keepsake.

Mildred Marie Wilson Dean was buried in Grant Memorial Park Cemetery in Marion six days after she died. Her parents, her in-laws, and Jimmy stood at the graveside. Winton was still in California. It is hard to understand why he did not go with his son and stand by his side during the funeral. He explained his absence later with these comments: "I was deep in debt with doctor's bills, X-rays, radium treatments and everything else. . . . I had to get my feet under me again."[23]

His parents and in-laws had paid for Grandma Emma and Jimmy's tickets and to have Mildred's remains shipped. It's likely the family would have paid for a ticket for Winton, too, if he had decided to go back home for the funeral. Instead, Winton sent Jimmy to the funeral on his own.

In just a few days, Jimmy had lost his mother and his father. For all practical purposes he was an orphan. Now, the nine-year-old faced a new life in a new home on the Winslows' farm in Fairmount, Indiana.

Chapter 4

Orphaned

Jimmy moved into the Winslows' fourteen-room house. It sat on a small hill surrounded by three hundred acres of land. His grandparents, Charles and Emma Dean, lived a few miles away in Fairmount. On his first day there, Aunt Ortense remembered that Jimmy ran all over the house, checking to make sure nothing had changed. Jimmy showed little emotion. Cousin Joan said: "He shut it all inside him. The only person he could ever have talked with was lying there in the coffin."[1]

Everyone felt sorry for him, and they did everything they could to help him adjust.[2] Someone gave Jimmy a pony, and Joan let him ride her bicycle. When he said he liked the Winslows' bedroom furniture, they moved it into his room. They made sure Jimmy got everything fourteen-year-old Joan did—and more.

Farm and Family

That summer, the family helped Jimmy get to know his new home. They told him about the American Indians who had first settled the land. He discovered trails, campsites, and pottery shards in the woods and fields near his new home. Jimmy learned to swim and fish in the pond. He played on the swing Marcus hung from a big tree in the yard. He adopted the runt of a litter of pigs and bottle fed it. The pig became his pet. When Jimmy ran across the farmyard, the little pig trotted along after him, squealing, trying to catch up.

Jimmy was invited to lend a hand with farm chores, but only if he wanted to. He helped milk the cows, gather the eggs, and feed the animals. He was a big help to Marcus, but in his own way. Later, Jimmy remembered how he did chores. "My uncle's place was a real farm, and I worked like crazy—as long as someone was watching me. Forty acres of oats made a huge stage, and when the audience left, I took a nap and nothing got plowed or harrowed."[3]

Jimmy was fascinated by the farm machinery. Whenever Marcus bought a new piece of equipment, "he had to know all about it,"[4] Ortense remembered. Once he had it all figured out, he lost interest.

Cousin Joan said: "He never was one to sit still."[5] Once he rigged up an elevator at the top of the Winslows' barn and almost broke his back testing it. Another time, he imitated a trapeze artist swinging on a rope. Jimmy fell to the barn floor and knocked out his four front teeth. He had to be fitted with a bridge. From then on, he loved to surprise guests by spitting out two of his false teeth and pretending he had just coughed out a few real teeth.[6]

When Jimmy was disobedient, his aunt and uncle scolded him, but halfheartedly, and rarely took away privileges. They never spanked him. Even surrounded by his Indiana family, Jimmy felt lonely. He missed his mother and could not understand why his father had abandoned him.[7] The distance between them grew a few months later. The United States entered World War II in 1941, and Jimmy's father was drafted into the Army Medical Corps. From then on, Jimmy called the Winslows Mom and Dad. He copied his uncle's mannerisms, wearing a T-shirt and blue jeans. He even slouched a bit when he walked, just like Marcus.

His grandmother, Emma, also remembered how Jimmy imitated his grandfather Dean. He would cross and uncross his legs just like his granddad did. He would march along behind the elderly gent, mimicking every movement. "It was more than a child's playful mocking," she said. "Even then, Jimmy seemed to be able to be another person."[8]

In 1943, three years after Jimmy came to live with the Winslows, Ortense gave birth to her second child, Marcus, Jr. Jimmy had to entertain himself while Ortense cared for baby Markie. He often looked at pictures in a family photo album or sketched with crayons. He drew cars, trucks, and farm machinery. His aunt encouraged Jimmy's love of art. She sent him to special art classes.

Small Town Boy

Growing up in Fairmount influenced Jimmy's childhood years. The small Indiana town, population twenty-six hundred, had changed little since the turn of the century. The business district covered two blocks along Main Street. There was a weekly newspaper, a volunteer fire department, elementary, junior, and senior high schools, a railroad depot, fifteen churches, a few glass factories, and one movie theater. The town was surrounded by some of the richest farmland in America. Fields were planted with corn, barley, oats, and wheat. Fairmount, the town that James Dean considered home, was also the birthplace of the hamburger, the ice-cream cone, and the automobile.

Jimmy "was sometimes moody, and often stubborn."

Jimmy's grades were poor in California, but they improved at Fairmount Elementary. One of his teachers, India Nose, recalled that Jimmy "was sometimes moody, and often stubborn. He could be forgetful too, as if he were lost in a daze." One day, during arithmetic class, Jimmy burst into tears in front of all the other children. When his teacher asked what he was crying about, he replied, "I miss my mother."[9] Though he seemed happy much of the time, Jimmy was the new kid in town. Everyone else at school knew one another. He felt isolated. Like many farm kids during that time, he went home after school to help with chores instead of playing with classmates.

Back in the Act

Fairmount had a historian named Bing Traster. He had won medals as the "World's Champion Liar." Jimmy followed Traster around and loved listening to his long-winded, animated stories.

Jimmy imitated the town historian and told tall tales like this one to friends:

> I remember one time when I found out that if you give a duck a piece of salt pork, it goes right through him in about ten seconds. So I got me some fishing line and tied a piece of pork to one end and fed it to a big drake. It passed on through and I gave it to another duck and then another, and before long I had the whole barnyard full of ducks all strung together like pearls on a string. You should have heard them quack.[10]

Jimmy discovered a collection of books filled with stories like those his mother read to him. The characters he liked best were the notorious outlaws like Butch Cassidy and America's fastest gunslinger, Harry Longabaugh, better known as the Sundance Kid. Jimmy acted out the train robberies, bank holdups, shootings, and other daring escapades of the outlaws. His favorite character was Billy the Kid. He first learned about him in school in California. Billy had also lost a parent. Jimmy always wrapped up a performance by saying that Billy was "just a kid" and not as wild as all the accounts reported.

Jimmy entertained his family with skits like those he and his mother had improvised. He quickly learned this was another way to get attention. When he got into his act, Jimmy disappeared. He *became* his character. His gift for make-believe made his audience laugh one moment and cry the next. The Winslows soon realized that their nephew had "a real talent for making you share his emotions."[11]

A Drama Coach

Ortense encouraged fourteen-year-old Jimmy to participate in a dramatic speaking contest in 1945. It was sponsored by the Women's Christian Temperance Union (WCTU), a group his aunt supported. Members of the WCTU believed in total abstinence, that no one should drink alcoholic beverages. Jimmy competed for the WCTU's highest award, the Pearl Medal.

Adeline Brookshire, the high-school speech and drama teacher, agreed to coach him. She remembered when he started seventh grade. "Even then I recognized the talent of this gifted boy," she said.

The teacher and student set to work on "Bars," the tale of a drunk who kills another man, then regrets his actions when jailed. They decided to use a chair with rungs in its back as a prop. Jimmy could sit on it and use the top of its back as a bar. He could also hold on to the vertical rungs like a man in a jail cell.

The day of the event, the judges refused to let Jimmy use the chair. The contest rules did not allow props. Without it, he stood in the middle of the stage, refusing to say a thing. When escorted off the platform, Jimmy did not apologize or cry. He threw a temper tantrum and blamed Brookshire for ruining his chances to win the prize. He refused to talk to her for weeks.[12]

In 1945, World War II ended and Winton Dean was discharged from the army. He came to Fairmount for a visit with a new wife, Ethel Case. They stayed for a week, and Jimmy spent as little time as possible around the farm until his father and new stepmother went back to California.

Sports, Motorbikes, and New Experiences

As Jimmy grew older, he explored different avenues to win approval and encouragement. He went out for sports in high school He excelled at baseball, basketball, and track, but was difficult to coach. Jimmy "couldn't take criticism in front of others," his high-school coach remembered.[13]

The young man put less energy into his studies. One report card Jimmy took home in 1948 showed a D⁻ in English, and C⁻ in American history, geometry, and safe driving. The only A he received was in art.

During high school, Jimmy made a faceless clay figure four inches high, with the head and body slumped forward. He showed it to Reverend James A. De Weerd, a local minister Jimmy admired. De Weerd asked him what the statue represented. Jimmy imitated the pose of the clay figure and said, "It's me. I call it 'self.'"[14]

Reverend De Weerd sponsored a group of boys Jimmy's age. He took them to the art museum in Indianapolis, encouraged them to write poetry, and showed them films of exotic lands and dancers. He introduced Jimmy to bongo drums, bullfighting, yoga, classical music, and literature. He told him, "The more things you know how to do and the more things you experience, the better off you'll be."[15] De Weerd also took his young friend to the Indianapolis 500, inspiring Jimmy's enthusiasm for car racing.

In 1947, Jimmy got his first motorcycle, a birthday gift from Ortense and Marcus. He painted the bike gold and black, his high-school colors. As he rode back and forth to Fairmount High, he always had the throttle wide open, hitting speeds of fifty miles per hour. He earned the nickname One-Speed Dean. The motorcycle shop near the farm became his second home. Its owner, Marvin Carter, remembered Jimmy's love of speed and his complete lack of fear. "If he had fallen only once," Carter mused, "things might have been different. Trouble is, he never got hurt. . . ."[16]

In 1947, Jimmy got his first motorcycle.

Every weekend, a small group of boys collected at Carter's Cycle Shop. They worked on their bikes and raced around a dirt track on the lot across from the shop. One day, Jimmy asked if he could use the shop's loudspeaker and he launched into an imaginary race. One of the boys remembered that "he'd get us all lined up, tell us what kind of weather it was, who got the jump, who crashed at the first turn, whose motorcycle was bursting into flames . . . he made it sound so real, I had to look twice to make sure I wasn't really racing."[17]

Senior Year and Graduation

In the spring of 1948, a new high-school principal asked students to write a short autobiography, and James Dean turned in "My Case Study." He wrote the assignment on lined notebook paper and said this about his future: "I think my life will be devoted to art and dramatics. . . . I got it and I know if I better myself then there will be no match. A fellow must have confidence."[18]

During junior high Jimmy developed a serious interest in acting. He performed in school and church plays. One of the plays was called *To Them That Sleep in Darkness*. Jimmy played a blind boy, and Grandma Emma said, "I wished he wasn't quite so good at it. I cried all the way through."[19]

As a senior, Jimmy starred in most of the school's productions. He played a monstrous Frankenstein in a spoof called *Goon With the Wind*. He earned a smaller role in *You Can't Take It With You*. As the mad Russian ballet master Kolenkhov, he bounded about the stage energetically, and even threw in a bit of Russian dancing. After one school production, the cast gave Adeline Brookshire, who was now married and had taken the name Adeline Nall, an orchid. The next morning, Jimmy asked to borrow the flower but would not tell his teacher why. Later, he returned the orchid along with a painting he had made of the blossom, explaining that now she would have it forever. He signed it: "Her Pride." Nall treasured the painting and kept it as long as she lived.

It is now on display at the Fairmount Historical Society for visitors to enjoy.

Before graduation, Jimmy made the front page of the *Fairmount News*. He won first place in a dramatic speaking contest in Peru, Indiana. He dramatized *A Madman's Manuscript* found in Chapter Eleven of Charles Dickens's *Pickwick Papers*. It recounts the story of a man who kills his wife after driving her insane. Next stop was the National Forensic League's finals in Colorado at the end of April where he represented Indiana in the contest. Fairmount raised the money to send Jimmy and his coach, Adeline Brookshire Nall, to Longmont, fifty miles north of Denver.

"Jimmy was wonderful," said Nall. "He would be very crazy and the next minute perfectly sane just like an adjustable lunatic. . . . It was a monologue but it had about as many emotions as you could use in a reading. You never get more than five or six characters in a reading, and he had at least that many moods and voice changes."[20]

In the first round, Jimmy received a good critique, but in the second round, judges told him the selection was too long. Nall had tried to talk Jimmy into shortening the twelve-minute piece. He refused, but he still shouted at her when he only placed sixth. He was angry that she didn't force him to shorten his piece.[21]

In his senior yearbook, Jimmy was saluted as a "brilliant guard in basketball." His teachers remembered him as a gifted student who lacked ambition. They did

James Dean in his senior yearbook photo.

not understand his dreams. His mother's death still haunted him. But the graduate no longer asked why she had left him. Now he had something to tell her: "I'm gonna show you! I'm gonna show you! I'm gonna be great!"[22]

"It was becoming plain to all of us that acting was the thing Jimmy was best at," Grandmother Dean said. After graduation, he decided to go to Los Angeles, live with his father, and study theater arts. Cousin Joan threw a going away party, and one day later, on June 15, 1949, James Dean waved good-bye to Fairmount, family, and friends.

Chapter 5

Early Acting Jobs

Eighteen-year-old James Dean took a bus from Chicago to California. This was his first trip back to the city where his mother had died. Dean had spent little time with his father during the last ten years, and he was uneasy about the reunion.[1]

Winton Dean was pleased his son was coming home. He wanted to build a relationship with him.[2] During the first few weeks, he took James bowling and tried to teach him how to play golf. He also bought him a 1939 Chevy. Winton encouraged his son to enroll at the Santa Monica City College. He approved of the curriculum it offered in physical education, teaching, and law. All were courses one could use to earn a living.

Though his father frowned on his desire to be an actor, James Dean volunteered at the Miller Playhouse. It was a summer stock company in Santa Monica. He painted scenery, worked as a stage manager, and performed. He adopted the stage name, Byron James. That was the only time he used a stage name.

In September, Dean followed his father's suggestion and enrolled in pre-law courses at Santa Monica College. He also signed up for two theater classes that Gene Nielsen Owens taught. Owens spotted Dean's talent. She also noticed that "his articulation was poor, he mashed his words. . . ."[3] At first, Owen blamed Dean's Hoosier accent. But the real problem was the plate holding his false front teeth in place. It made tongue positions for certain sounds difficult. Owens and Dean "launched a semester-long . . . oral interpretation of Hamlet. I told him that if anything would clear up fuzzy speech it would be the demanding soliloquies of Shakespeare," she said.[4]

During the year, Dean got A's in gym and drama and C's in his pre-law classes. The grades showed his true interests. After one year at Santa Monica, he decided to transfer to the University of California Los Angeles (UCLA) and major in theater arts.

That summer, Dean coached boys at a local military academy. He saved what he earned for tuition and then spent most of the money on a trip home to see relatives and friends. While in Indiana, he saw Marlon Brando make his screen debut in the newly-released movie, *The Men*. Dean was impressed by the intensity of Brando's acting. He appreciated the hard work and dedication required to perfect such a performance. He learned Brando had spent weeks living in the paraplegic ward of a military hospital before filming began. The experience helped Brando realistically portray the feelings of a soldier who had lost the use of his legs and was confined to a wheelchair. Dean also identified with Brando, a rebel who refused to conform to the expectations of Hollywood movie big shots.[5]

University of California Los Angeles

Dean landed a part in the university production of *Macbeth* during his first month at UCLA. Another theater arts student, William (Bill) Bast, watched his performance during a final dress rehearsal. Bast was unimpressed with the kid on stage. "James Dean," he said to himself, "a name to forget."[6]

Later, Bast's girlfriend, Beverly Wills, took him backstage and introduced the two young men. Bast recalled that Dean seemed to be "nothing more than a simple, withdrawn, little boy, not too long off the farm,"[7] but they discovered common ground. Both grew up in the Midwest and both were theater arts students. This was the opening act in a close friendship.

The curtain went up on *Macbeth*, but Dean's debut was not a success. The review in the faculty newsletter said that he "failed to show any growth and would have made a hollow king."[8] One person in the audience did see a spark in Dean's performance. Talent scout Isabel Draesmer felt he delivered his closing speech with a natural power and passion. She went backstage after the performance and told Dean to call her if he ever wanted an agent. He made an appointment a few days later.

Dean pledged Sigma Nu, a fraternity, when he enrolled at UCLA. He lived in the fraternity house, but he quickly discovered he did not fit in with the group. His fraternity brothers teased him about being an actor. He lost his temper when they made snide jokes about "actors, fruits, and ballerinas."[9] He punched two of them, and the fraternity threw him out. He left without paying a forty-five-dollar bill for rent and now had to find another place to stay.

Bast was also unhappy with his living arrangements in the dorm. Dean asked if he wanted to share an apartment. When Bast agreed, Dean was so ecstatic that he began describing his dreams and aspirations:

> All I know is, I've got to do something. I don't know exactly what it is yet. . . . I've got to keep trying until I hit the right thing. . . . It's like I want to be an actor, but that isn't it. . . . Just being an actor or a director, even a good one, isn't enough. . . . To me, the only success, the only greatness for man, is immortality. To have your work remembered in history, to leave something in this world that will last for centuries. That's greatness. . . . [10]

Roommate and Friend

Dean and Bast found a three-room apartment. The rent was more than they could afford, but they took it anyway. Bast remembered how the decision was made. Dean strutted through the three rooms. He sat on all the furniture, tried out the shower and toilet. He opened and closed the refrigerator, oven, and every cupboard door. He stood outside on the sundeck, studied the ocean view, then sat down in the middle of the floor and announced that he planned to live right there in "the penthouse," as they dubbed the apartment that occupied the top floor of a three-story house.

The first month's rent took all their money. To pay for their new place, Bast found a job as an usher at the CBS studios. He also picked up small parts in radio productions. Bast helped Dean find parts in CBS Radio workshop dramas, too. Dean introduced Bill to Draesmer. The agent agreed to represent both young actors.

As they settled into the routine of living together, Bast soon realized that Dean was more than a little moody. When things were not going well, Dean sulked silently. He refused to talk to anyone. This could go on for two or three days at a time. Then, just as suddenly, he and Bast would again be best friends.[11] Bill never knew which Dean he would find when he arrived home.

Commercials and Bit Parts

Dean followed up leads from his agent and worked hard to find parts on his own. He read the *Daily Variety* and *Hollywood Reporter*, papers that kept tabs on the movie industry. He called on producers and casting directors. He showed up for tryouts. When he did not get a part he auditioned for, he refused to talk about it. Another young actor offered this observation about Dean and his peers: "When you don't get a part, you and the other people get together and discuss why you didn't get it, and you try to be objective. But Dean, after losing [a] part, just kind of clammed up and had nothing to do with anybody. I knew he was angry, heartsick about it. And then he just kind of took off."[12]

Draesmer got Dean his first professional acting job in 1951. It was a two-minute Coca-Cola® commercial. The Coke people needed all-American teenagers and paid ten dollars a day. The first day of filming was in Griffith Park on the merry-go-round. Dean was instructed to hand frosty twelve-ounce bottles to kids as they spun in and out of the picture on the carousel horses. The best performers from that shoot were selected for a second day of work. Dean was one of them. "The director spotted Jimmy," said a crew member, "and took a lot of close-ups of him. . . . They wanted action and reaction and I guess he came through as the best."[13]

Soon after that, the same director cast Dean as John the Baptist in an Easter television special called *Hill Number One*. His role was small, but Dean agonized during the rehearsals and shootings. Bast watched his roommate's depression with concern. "I had never known such lack of communication. . . . He would sit in his room . . . and stare into space for hours. I made several attempts to get through to him, but rarely got more than a grunt or a distant stare for a response."[14]

When *Hill Number One* aired, Dean handled his small part to his credit.

High-school Fan Club

His role as John the Baptist impressed one particular audience, the girls of the Immaculate Heart High School. They had been instructed to watch the film for homework during Easter vacation. The James Dean fans contacted his agent and invited Dean to a tea party at school. Bast went with his friend and reported that "a lot of giggling went on. . . . The girls were between fourteen and eighteen. It was one of those embarrassing affairs where everyone just stands around a lot. Dean got to play the star to the hilt and he loved it."[15]

No other offers of work followed *Hill Number One* and Dean's money soon ran out. He was depressed and could not sleep. Late at night, he would walk to the Venice Amusement Pier and hang out with alcoholics and street people until dawn. One Los Angeles realtor remembers seeing Dean: "He looked like a teenage hobo. He used to stand around . . . with a hangdog look, or he'd be walking around eating a hot dog, just walking back and forth along the beach strip."[16] Bast found it easiest to ignore his roommate when he sunk into these moods.

To pay his share of the rent, Bast helped Dean get a part-time usher job with CBS Radio studios. Dean enjoyed watching the shows, but he did not like being told what to do and what to wear.[17] He called the uniform a "monkey suit." He was fired at the end of the first week.

Gals and Guys

By January 1951, after one semester at UCLA, Dean dropped most of his classes. He focused on auditions, trying to win some bit parts to pay for rent and food. Bast was covering most of their expenses. He even paid for the gas to run Dean's car. Dean's moods made it more and more difficult to room with him. Bast ignored him as much as he could, but when his roommate stole his girlfriend, Beverly Wills, daughter of comedienne Joan Davis, that was the final blow. Bast moved out.

For a while, Dean managed to stay in the apartment, borrowing money from Beverly to pay the rent by himself. Then, he landed a job parking cars at a lot next to the CBS studios. It suited him perfectly. He did not have to wear a uniform, the hours were easy, and there was a chance the young actor might park the car of an executive who could further his career.

Dean met Rogers Brackett on the job. Brackett was an account executive with an advertising agency. He knew the right people in Hollywood. He was also homosexual. Brackett took an interest in Dean, offering to help the actor. Within weeks, Dean broke up with his girlfriend and moved into Brackett's apartment on Sunset Plaza Drive. He told friends that his live-in situation with the older man was his meal ticket, but Brackett later said, "If it was a father-son relationship, it was also incestuous," hinting that he had a sexual relation with the young actor.[18] Dean described one incident to girlfriend Dizzy Sheridan that implied he and Brackett had at least one sexual encounter. However, Brackett's suggestion of a live-in relationship is often questioned.

Brackett took Dean to parties, private screenings, and dinners. He helped the aspiring actor make contact with others in the industry. The two took several trips to Mexico to see bullfights. During one trip, Brackett introduced Dean to director Budd Boetticher. He was making a movie called *The Bullfighter and the Lady*. The director liked Dean and gave him a cape used by Sidney Franklin, a famous matador who grew up in Brooklyn, New York.

Brackett also gave Dean a copy of *The Little Prince*, by Antoine de Saint-Exupéry. The book became his favorite. Dean read it often and quoted passages from it to friends.[19]

During the next couple of months, the advertising executive also got the young actor bit parts in three movies. Now Dean had exciting news to share. He looked up his old roommate, Bill Bast, the only person he felt he could talk to. The two patched up their differences and were once again on friendly terms.

Actor's Workshop

Bast had organized an actors' study group under the direction of James Whitmore. Whitmore was a member of the Actors Studio in New York. He had worked under Lee Strasberg and Elia Kazan. Dean attended the workshops with Bast and several other students serious about acting. Early exercises consisted of basic movements and mimes. During more advanced sessions, the director set up imaginary situations between two actors and turned them loose to improvise.

Bast and Dean did one scene together. Bast was a jeweler trying to delay a thief until the police arrived.

Dean, the thief, needed to reclaim a stolen watch he had left with the jeweler for repairs and escape. After several unsuccessful trials, Whitmore worked with Dean individually. Then the two actors tried the scene again. This time, Dean became the thief so completely that even his appearance changed. He abused "the jeweler" until Bast lost his temper. The two were ready to throw punches at each other before they finished.[20]

The exercise required an intense amount of emotional energy. It took Dean time to release the nervous excitement created by his performance. Then he slipped into a depression. His difficulty unwinding after pouring all his emotions into an intense acting scene was a problem he faced throughout his career.[21]

Dean later complimented Whitmore for his help and advice. "I owe a lot to him. . . . He told me I didn't know the difference between acting as a soft job, and acting as a difficult art. I needed to learn the difference."[22]

Whitmore also advised Dean to go to New York, to test his abilities on stage, and become a member of the Actors Studio. Dean was ready to put his ambitions and talents to work and decided to leave for New York that fall.

Bast learned secondhand that his friend had gone east. A telephone message left under his door relayed this message: "Mr. Dean called. Gone to New York."[23]

Chapter 6

The Big City

Two and a half years out of high school, James Dean felt ready to tackle the next step in his career but did not have the money to pay for a cross-country move. He took advantage of the fact that Brackett's agency had transferred the account executive to New York. They decided to travel east together. They left California in early October 1951, and Brackett paid most of the expenses. The account executive first stopped in Chicago where he had a directing assignment. Dean took the train to Fairmount for a short visit with his family. He also went to see Reverend De Weerd in Indianapolis. His old friend gave him two hundred dollars to fund his traveling expenses, and Dean went on to New York alone.

Dean arrived at Grand Central Station and called Alec Wilder. Brackett knew the composer and asked him to help Dean get settled. Wilder took him to breakfast and then found him a room at the modestly priced Hotel Iroquois on Forty-fourth Street.

Dean remembered his first reaction to the city. "New York overwhelmed me. For the first few weeks I only strayed a couple of blocks from my hotel off Times Square. I would see three movies a day in an attempt to escape my loneliness and depression. I spent $150 of my limited funds just on seeing movies."[1]

As his funds ran low, Dean worried about his prospects.[2] He had trouble sleeping and roamed the streets at all hours of the night. He drank enormous amounts of coffee and smoked and drank alcohol. To stretch his limited budget, he searched for the best low-priced places to eat in New York. Dean dined at Horn and Hardart's chain of automats. Food was displayed behind small windowed doors. A coin fed into a slot opened the window, allowing a customer to remove the food. Dean also made friends with the owner of Jerry's Bar on Sixth Avenue at Fifty-fourth Street. Jerry Lucci often gave the starving actor something to eat at no charge. Another hangout for Dean was Cromwell's Pharmacy. Actors could sit for hours at the coffee counter, only getting up once in a while to make calls to their agents.

Beat the Clock

Dean's situation improved when Brackett sent him to see James Sheldon. Sheldon supervised commercials for a New York advertising firm. He found Dean moody but likeable.[3] He introduced him to agent Jane Deacy. Deacy and Dean liked each other immediately.[4] The agent saw a talented young man who needed gentle encouragement

James Dean sits at the counter of Cromwell's Pharmacy in New York in the early 1950s.

and direction. Dean found a stand-in mother and even called her Mom.

Deacy got him a job as a rehearsal stuntman for the weekly game show, *Beat the Clock*. To win prizes contestants had to perform stunts in a race against time. The wacky stunts included juggling plates while standing on one foot or transferring water from one glass to another using a straw. It was Dean's responsibility to test the activities, a job he did too well. The job paid five dollars an hour, earning him about sixty dollars a week. Unfortunately, no contestant could perform stunts as quickly and skillfully as Dean, so he was fired and lost a steady income.

Next Dean tried out for a part on a popular television sitcom, *Mama*. After auditioning, he was offered the job on the spot, and it looked as if he had his big break. He would replace Dick Van Patten, who was about to be drafted. Unfortunately, the opportunity did not materialize. The draft board rejected Van Patten and he returned to the television series.

Romance With Dizzy

On a rainy afternoon in January 1952, Dean made a new friend. Her name was Elizabeth Sheridan, but friends called her Dizzy. Today she is known for her role on *Seinfeld*. Liz Sheridan played Jerry's mother in the TV sitcom.

When she met Dean, Sheridan was an aspiring dancer struggling to make it on her own. She enjoyed talking with Dean and invited him to watch her perform at a Harlem club. He went and was impressed.[5] The dancer was two years older, but admired Dean's ambition and clever doodling. The two shared a quick sense of humor and spent nights hanging out in bars and cafes. During the day, they walked around Central Park and danced along Broadway.

Soon their friendship turned to love, and they moved into an apartment on West Seventy-first Street together. "We clung together that year, for a lot of reasons—not the least being that it was the first time both of us were really falling for someone."[6] Dizzy remembered that Dean seemed to have no roots, was full of pent-up energy, and was looking for a place to call home. They talked about his mother, and Dean told her he believed Mildred's spirit was part of him.[7] Sheridan said Dean had little to say about his father, Winton.

Dizzy remembered that Dean seemed to have no roots, was full of pent-up energy, and was looking for a place to call home.

For the next few months, Dean and Dizzy encouraged each other. They laughed together, discussed bullfighting, art history, music, and poetry. They spent many evenings reading *The Little Prince*. This fable tells the adventures of a visitor from outer space as he discovers the true meaning of friendship. Dean read favorite lines aloud to Dizzy, "It is only with the heart that one can see rightly; what is essential is invisible to the eye." Dean saw himself as a little prince, a lonely outsider. He wanted to be like the title character and refuse to do anything earthbound.[8]

In spite of all the fun they shared, life was a struggle for the young couple. Supper was often a bowl of shredded wheat. As Dizzy said, "[H]alf the time we seemed on the edge of starvation."[9] She went from one dance job to another and also worked part-time retouching photos.

Dean picked up a few bit parts and even one lead in a play written for television. He also began to earn a reputation. He frequently showed up for rehearsals, according to one director, "very badly dressed . . . he was absolutely impossible to work with, arrogant and uncooperative . . . until he went on the air . . . and then he was absolutely brilliant."[10]

The Winslows bought their first television set to watch Dean perform in "Sleeping Dogs." The program aired on February 20, 1952. Ortense thought her nephew looked too thin. The Winslows immediately shipped him a box of canned goods and included a check with orders to go grocery shopping.

Old Connections

That spring, Dean and Dizzy split for a while when Brackett finally arrived in New York. Dean explained how Brackett had helped his career. He wanted to renew their friendship. He knew the older man's connections could still open doors.

Dean also told Dizzy about their trip from Los Angeles to Chicago. Brackett had made a pass at him, Dean said. "He didn't threaten me or anything, but he gave me the impression that our relationship depended on that moment. I decided to go along with it. I succumbed to him. I felt bad afterward. . . . I felt really strange selling myself like that, so I left him in Chicago . . . and came to New York on my own."[11]

Dizzy moved out. Dean spent more time again with Brackett but was secretive about their relationship. He did not want anyone to suggest that he and Brackett were sexual partners. Movie and television studios strictly enforced their morals clauses. Homosexuality was considered immoral.[12] Many public figures kept their sexual inclinations a secret. If discovered, the studios would blacklist them, ending their careers.

Later, Dizzy said she did not believe Dean wanted to be gay. However, he was drawn to unconventional behavior and willing to experiment.[13]

Television Bits

Early television programs were performed for live audiences. Studios rushed to fill air time. Scripts were often poorly written and programs produced too quickly. The acting was usually bad. Actors earned little for television bit parts, but these roles allowed talent scouts an opportunity to see how they came across on camera.

Dean's talents were spotted in May 1952. He was cast as William Scott in a production titled "Abraham Lincoln." In the drama, Scott, a soldier from Vermont, was to be court-martialed for falling asleep on night watch during the Civil War. During rehearsals, Dean was uncooperative and withdrawn. Once the show began, he breathed life into his character. In one scene, the young soldier wept quietly not out of fear for his life but out of shame. He felt he had disgraced his widowed mother. Lincoln saw the boy's sense of honor and pardoned him. Dean's performance as Scott showed that he could portray deeply emotional scenes in a natural way for the camera.

The Actors Studio

That fall, Dean met Christine White, an aspiring playwright. He invited her for coffee and the two talked for hours. They both wanted to audition for the Actors Studio. Dean suggested they use a scene from her play for the tryout. Together they revised, rewrote, and rehearsed everyday for the next five weeks.

On the day of the audition, more than one hundred hopeful artists showed up. As time neared for the two of them to take the stage, Dean got cold feet. He told White he was not doing the scene and nearly bolted from the auditorium before his partner convinced him to stay.

When the auditions were over, Elia Kazan, Lee Strasburg, and Cheryl Crawford selected twelve finalists. Of the twelve, only James Dean and Christine White were invited to join the Actors Studio. Dean wrote home telling the Winslows of his success: " . . . I am very proud to announce that I am a member of the Actors Studio. The greatest school of the theatre. . . . It is the best thing that can happen to an actor. I am one of the youngest to belong."[14]

Dean was proud to be part of the school, but his first

solo presentation at the Actors Studio was his last. Strasberg tore apart the scene he adapted from a novel called *Matador*. The director harshly criticized Dean in front of the entire class, so everyone could learn from his mistakes.[15] This was Strasberg's method, one that had earned him his reputation as a great teacher. Dean still could not accept being critiqued and stormed out. Later he said:

> If I let them dissect me like a rabbit in a clinical research laboratory I might not be able to produce again. . . . That man had no right to tear me down like that. You keep knocking a guy down and you'll take the guts away from him. And what's an actor without guts.[16]

Strasberg later explained that he only examined a scene so intensely when an actor showed he truly had underlying talent. Dean continued to attend sessions at the Actor's Studio but only as part of the audience. He never subjected himself again to Strasberg's critique.

Back Home Again in Indiana

In May, Bill Bast moved to New York to find work as a writer. He looked Dean up, and in spite of their experiences in Los Angeles, the two friends decided to room together again. Dean and Dizzy were back together, too, and in October 1952, the three moved into a dingy little apartment. Jobs were not rolling in for any of them. Money was tight. They barely had enough to pay rent. Food was a luxury. Dean suggested they leave their problems behind and hitchhike to Indiana to visit the Winslows. "You'd both love it. It's all clean and fresh, lots of trees and open fields. Tons of good food, chicken and steak, all that jazz."[17] On that note the three friends set out for Indiana.

The Winslows welcomed Dean, Bill, and Dizzy. They were quickly invited to sit down to a hearty farm meal. Later, Dean showed his friends his hometown. He talked farming with his Uncle Marcus and played with his cousin, Markie.

The director told him to get his glasses fixed and come back.

Adeline Nall invited them to address her high-school drama class. Bill talked about writing. Dizzy demonstrated dance as another form of communication. Dean recited one sentence: "My name is James Dean and I am an actor."[18] He did it over and over in a dozen different ways, including forlornly, hysterically, hostilely, and tearfully. He also told students that Nall was the best teacher he ever had.

As the trio were about to accept the Winslows' invitation to stay longer, Dean's agent called. He had to return to New York immediately. He had been asked to read for the part of Wally Wilkins, a tormented seventeen-year-old in the Broadway production, *See the Jaguar*.

Broadway Debut

Dean's first tryout for the play did not go well. He arrived with one lens of his glasses cracked. Since he could hardly see the script, he read poorly. The director told him to get his glasses fixed and come back. He even gave Dean ten dollars when the young actor explained that he had no money.

Two days later, Dean was back, but his glasses were still broken. The director asked him to explain. Dean pulled a hunting knife from his pocket. "I just had to have it," he said, "but I figured I couldn't betray you entirely so I memorized the script."[19] He was prepared this time, and a week later Dean had the part of Wally in *See the Jaguar*.

For the most part, Dean cooperated with the director and cast. He only had one incident during rehearsals. He got into an argument and pulled his knife on a cast member. Another actor broke up the fight. He took the knife away, snapping the blade in two. Dean was warned that violence would not be tolerated.

On opening night, Bast watched from the audience:

> I was stunned by the realization that at no time during the performance had I been aware that I was watching my friend James Dean. He had so completely created an illusion for me and the rest of the audience that I had believed in Wally Wilkins, the part he was playing, not Jimmy Dean the boy I knew.[20]

Unfortunately, critics panned the play and *See the Jaguar* closed after only five performances. Dean did receive good reviews for his role. One called his performance "extraordinary . . . in an almost impossible role."[21]

Shortly after the Broadway show closed, Bast took a writing job in Los Angeles. Sheridan's work took her to

Trinidad, and she did not see Dean for two years. She later wrote that she always remembered:

> the little-boy side of Jimmy—his high giggles, his love of animals, his sweetness with children and older people, his passion to learn everything quickly, before it was too late to learn anything. And . . . his need to be loved—an infinite need. . . . He was like a bottomless well. No matter how much anyone or everyone offered, no love was enough.[22]

A Lonely Christmas

That Christmas, the Winslows offered to send money so Dean could come home, but he stayed in New York. He bought himself a Christmas present, a recorder, a flutelike woodwind instrument. During the holidays he often sat alone at his hotel window. "Being an actor is the loneliest thing in the world," he said. "You're all alone with your imagination, and that's all you have."[23]

Chapter 7

Discovered

During 1953, Dean's prospects brightened. His agent found him enough work to keep him busy. He was earning money and paying his own way. He appeared in a number of television shows. These included episodes of *Danger*, *Kraft Television Theater*, and *U.S. Steel Hour*. He also appeared in the season premiere of *Omnibus*, hosted by Alistair Cooke.

Hip teenagers were featured in many new dramas, creating parts for young characters. Dean regularly competed with two other actors, Paul Newman and Steve McQueen, for juvenile leads.[1] Most television dramas Dean appeared in are gone forever. In the 1950s, TV material was not preserved. However, the studios did save some shows Dean made after he became a movie star.

From what is remembered of his roles, Dean was often typecast. He portrayed frustrated teens or crazed killers. One week Dean would be a confused murderer

This photo shows Dean with Patrick Knowles in the *U.S. Steel Hour* production of "The Thief."

on the run, the next a beatnik assassin, or a mentally disturbed janitor. His best performance was in a Rod Serling production for the *Kraft Television Theater*, called "A Long Time Till Dawn." Dean played Joe Harris, a boy just released from prison who did not get along with his father. Serling said, "There was an excitement and intensity about him [Dean] that he transmitted . . . to the audience."[2]

During this year, Dean built a reputation—a bad one. A warning label came with any recommendation to hire him: The kid had talent if it could be tapped and tamed.[3] During one filming session, Director Archer King instructed Dean to stay in the chalk lines on the set. Dean blew up: "I was trying to get a characterization. I couldn't worry about some damn chalk."[4]

Dean often interrupted the dry run of a scene to ask questions about his character's motive. This slowed production and irked directors. At the time, getting the job done quickly was the top priority. Directors were rewarded for the quantity, not the quality of television programs.

Director Andrew McCullough worked with the young actor on two projects. He remembered the complaints of experienced actors. They disliked the way Dean never said the same line the same way twice. Dean amazed McCullough when he was cast opposite an eight-year-old girl.[5] His behavior toward her was gentle and thoughtful, almost fatherly.

Though warned that he was putting his career at

risk, Dean continued to play the "bad boy" during rehearsals. In fact, his behavior almost lost him one role. Dean arrived late as usual, showing disrespect for the actors and crew he kept waiting. He got upset during rehearsal, threw the script on the floor, and stormed off. After two more temper tantrums, the director threatened to fire him. One veteran actor spoke on Dean's behalf: "He's untutored but talented, and I think it's wrong for us to retard [restrict] him."[6] That comment saved Dean's job. When the show aired, Dean stole the spotlight giving an outstanding performance.

New Passions

Dean became a popular escort for young actresses. He had a brief affair with Betsy Palmer, who had grown up in Indiana. His longest relationship was with actress Barbara Glenn. They met at Cromwell's coffee counter and dated until he went to Hollywood in 1954. The two were always breaking up, then making up. They even discussed marriage at one point before their final split.

Dean was also spotted out on the town with actress Arlene Lorca (Sachs). She introduced him to photographer Roy Schatt. This meeting prompted Dean to buy a camera. He asked Schatt to show him how to use it, and the photographer taught him the basics. Dean enjoyed composing and taking pictures but found darkroom work tedious. At his first lesson on developing film, he exclaimed that it was too much work.[7] He just wanted to shoot the pictures. He took dance lessons with Eartha Kitt, bongo lessons from Cyril Jackson, and piano lessons from composer Leonard Rosenman. Dean dropped most of these hobbies as quickly as he took them up, but he never lost interest in photography or the bongo drums.

Show Biz in the Fifties

In 1953, fear of being labeled Communist influenced the television and movie studios. They stopped airing programs with controversial topics. It was the beginning of the Cold War, and Senator Joseph McCarthy of Wisconsin was on a witch hunt. No one was safe as McCarthy searched for Communists, real and imagined. He believed the movie and television industry shaped public opinions. He accused writers and performers of being Communists. Some were forced to flee the country to avoid being jailed. People's careers were destroyed. Dean did not want his name added to McCarthy's blacklist. He had little interest in politics and refused to discuss his view on issues with anyone.[8]

Dean now lived in one tiny room that had two round porthole shaped windows. The apartment was at the top of five narrow flights of stairs. Inside there was only enough space for a daybed, a built-in desk, and a hot plate. He decorated the walls with the bull horns and the cape that had belonged to the famous matador, Sidney Franklin. The place was usually a disaster, littered with empty beer cans and half-eaten food. Records and books were stacked everywhere.

Attracting Attention

Dean did things that shocked people. One night he moved an armchair from Ray Shatt's studio into the middle of a busy New York street. He sat down in it and blocked traffic.

Dean admired Montgomery Clift and Marlon Brando. He watched their movies repeatedly, trying to understand their techniques. When they attended Actors Studio sessions, he watched their every move. He followed them around town and even paid for their unlisted phone numbers. He called Montgomery Clift repeatedly.[9] When Clift answered, all the star heard was someone breathing on the other end. Clift changed his phone number to stop the calls. Dean also left messages on Brando's answering service, asking the star to call him back. Brando ignored the request.

Rumors were flying about the bisexuality of Marlon Brando and the homosexuality of Montgomery Clift. Despite fear of being censored, Dean tested the waters with partner Jonathan Gilmore. Gilmore remembered that Dean "wanted to be . . . a renegade and an outsider." Once he talked Gilmore into going to a party in Greenwich Village as his date, dressed as a woman. They staged an elaborate fight, in which Gilmore revealed he was a man in costume, then they kissed and made up.[10]

Lights on Broadway Again

In November 1954, Dean auditioned for a part in a Broadway play, *The Immoralist*. It was adapted from a novel written by Andre Gide and produced by Billy Rose. Dean won the role of Bachir, a young Arab houseboy. As the play opens, an archeologist and his bride arrive in Morocco on their honeymoon. The husband, who is a closet homosexual, meets the lecherous Bachir. In this role, Dean performed a seductive dance, luring the archeologist away from his bride and back to the gay world.

Unfortunately, the play was in trouble from the start. The director who hired Dean was fired. The new director, Daniel Mann, and Dean did not work well together. Mann said, "I would ask him to do what he had to do, try to communicate with him, but it was extremely difficult. He was a rebel."[11] Once when Mann reprimanded him for not playing a scene correctly, the young actor stubbornly replied. "I think I did all right."[12]

Sparks really flew when one week before opening night the producers made major cuts to the script, mostly to the part of Bachir. The last-minute changes upset Dean. He did get even, though, pulling one more stunt that angered Mann. Dean nearly missed the opening curtain for the play's first New York performance. He went out for a spin on his new Indian motorcycle and barely made it back in time.

The Immoralist opened on Dean's twenty-third birthday, February 8, 1954. The reviews of the play were encouraging. Once again, critics such as Walter Kerr and Richard Watts, Jr., applauded Dean as the play's shining star. The young actor's performance was a personal triumph.

Barbara Glenn remembered how Dean showed up for the cast party later that night. It was held at Sardi's, a fashionable New York restaurant. He came in torn jeans and a T-shirt and was turned away. Dean hopped on his motorcycle and roared back to his apartment on Sixty-eighth Street. He changed into a suit and tie and then came roaring back to celebrate. This was the one and only time Glenn remembered seeing Dean dressed up.

A Big Break

While rehearsals were underway for *The Immoralist*, Warner Bros. auditioned Dean and dozens of other young actors for roles in a war film, *Battle Cry*.

"I did the screen test for Jimmy," said William Orr, a top executive for the studio:

> He came in wearing these . . . "battle fatigues" . . . a dirty cap, days' worth of beard, dungarees. I told him we were going to do a gentle love scene between a soldier and his girlfriend, whose father doesn't like the boy. And without a bit of preparation, Jimmy Dean gave a reading that was the best I'd ever heard.[13]

Orr sent a glowing commendation to the Burbank Studios. "James Dean . . . is gaining quite a reputation as a fine young actor," he wrote. "There is a trace of the Marlon Brando school in his work."[14]

Dean did not win a role in this film, but he had

impressed Orr. Now he had high hopes of winning a prize part—one that was much bigger than Bachir.

Dean and Kazan

Elia Kazan had struck a deal with Warner Bros. to direct a new movie, *East of Eden*. Paul Osborn, another New Yorker, was hired to write the script. In February, the writer attended a rehearsal of *The Immoralist*. After seeing Dean as Bachir, Osborn suggested Kazan audition the young star for the role of Cal Trask. The director agreed and called Dean's agent. They set up an interview at Warner Bros.' New York office.

Kazan remembered his first meeting with Dean and wrote about it in his autobiography: "When I walked in he was slouched at the end of a leather sofa in the waiting room, a heap of twisted legs and denim rags, looking resentful for no particular reason. I didn't like the expression on his face, so I kept him waiting."[15]

When Kazan finally called the actor in to talk, Dean's attitude improved. Kazan recalled he was difficult to talk to, saying "conversation was not his gift."[16] Dean offered to take the older man on a motorcycle ride. Kazan accepted, and within minutes they were roaring down Broadway with Kazan perched on the seat behind Dean. The wild ride convinced him that the young actor was a show-off.

Kazan found little to like in Dean but realized he was perfect for the role of Cal.[17] He sent him to meet the author of the book, John Steinbeck. Steinbeck agreed with Kazan. Dean was Cal. Now all Dean had to do was perform well during the screen tests.

A date for the screen test was set. Paul Newman was being considered for the part of Aron. Dean arrived for the test dressed in a casual, open-neck shirt. Newman wore a dress shirt and bow tie. The two young actors performed side by side for director Kazan. They stood in front of the camera, ad-libbing as Kazan asked questions and gave them directions. Dean and Newman moved and turned, allowing the camera to catch them from all angles. By the end of the test, Dean had the part of Cal locked up.

Now his agent, Deacy, negotiated a deal that protected his interests. After Dean signed with Warner Bros., he still wanted to be able to work in television. While the details were being ironed out, Dean introduced Kazan to Leonard Rosenman. The twenty-nine-year-old was gaining a reputation as a composer. Dean suggested the director listen to a score Rosenman wrote.[18] Kazan liked what he heard. Rosenman, like Dean, made his film debut with the musical score for *East of Eden*.

A New Star

On February 20, just two weeks after opening night, Dean surprised everyone involved with *The Immoralist*. He resigned with no explanation. Twelve days later, his reason became clear. Warner Bros. made an announcement. James Dean would star in Elia Kazan's production of *East of Eden*. Dean had the break he had been waiting for.

Chapter 8

Lights, Camera, Action

Within two months time, Dean was on his way to Hollywood, the site of Warner Bros. Studios. While he waited for filming to begin, he used part of his seven-hundred-dollar advance from the studio to buy a red convertible sports car. Dean spent much of his time zooming around the city at high speeds. He also bought a motorcycle, though he could not ride it until the movie was completed. His contract specifically banned motorcycle riding. The studio did not want an accident to delay production.

Dean also bought a palomino horse called Cisco. He stabled the horse on the studio's back lot and often slipped away in the middle of shooting to feed the animal. This happened so often that Kazan finally insisted the horse be taken away. The actor moved Cisco to a ranch in the San Fernando Valley.

In late May 1954, the cast and crew began shooting in northern California. They were to spend three weeks

Dean loved cars and even entered car races.

near Mendocino and Salinas. It quickly became clear that working with Dean was going to challenge the director, the more-experienced actors, and the schedule. This was Dean's first picture. He had to learn how to prepare for the demanding work required on an hourly and daily basis. He "wasn't easy [to work with]," Kazan said, "because it was all new to him. But when he got the affection and patience he needed, he was awfully good. There wasn't anything he held back. He was loaded with talent, but he had very little training and he was ready to do anything to be good."[1]

Dean prepared in his own unique way. Whether the scene was small or large, he could not be rushed. It often took him an extremely long time to feel ready to give his best performance. Kazan was patient. He knew he needed Dean at his best. The other members of the cast and crew were forced to wait, too. In addition, the cast had to deal with another of the young actor's quirks. Dean could not or would not repeat his same performance during a retake of a scene.

Dean held up shooting one other time while on location. He came in contact with poison oak. He was confined to bed for several days waiting for the itchy, irritating welts to heal. Until he was well again, shooting came to a standstill.

Kazan learned a great deal about Dean during those days on location. He discovered how well the camera captured his expressive face and eyes. "You really felt so sorry for him when you saw him in close-up," the director said. . . . His body was more expressive . . . than [Marlon] Brando's—it had so much tension in it."[2]

The Cast

Kazan carefully selected all the leading roles for the cast of *East of Eden*. The role of Adam Trask was played by Raymond Massey, a conservative actor with strong religious beliefs. Massey seemed an odd choice to many, but Kazan knew exactly what he was doing. Dean and Massey clashed, just like the son and father in the script. Massey remembered Dean as "a rebel at heart, a boy who approached everything in the picture with a chip on his shoulder, was deliberately antisocial . . . simple technicalities, such as moving on cue and finding his marks, were beneath his consideration."[3]

Massey remembered Dean as "a rebel at heart, a boy who approached everything in the picture with a chip on his shoulder, was deliberately antisocial."

Massey studied the script nightly with his wife and memorized his lines precisely. He found it nearly impossible to work with Dean. He complained bitterly when the young actor cut in on someone's lines or said the wrong lines.[4] Kazan worked the tension created by the personality clash between them. He "let Jimmy say his lines the way he wanted—just because it irritated Massey!"[5] He did nothing to stop the antagonism. In fact, he did everything possible to increase it. Kazan respected Massey, but he realized that the actor's hostility toward Dean would produce a more powerful performance.

One famous scene in *East of Eden* is the Bible-reading scene. Cal's father makes his son read verses as punishment for destroying property. Cal infuriates his father by reading each verse number even though Adam instructs him not to. As the actors prepared to film this emotional scene, Kazan took Dean aside and told him to mutter obscenities instead of reciting the verses. He wanted to annoy Massey. Dean's cursing infuriated his religious costar. He shouted to Kazan, "You never know what he's going to do. Make him read the lines the way they're written."[6] With this little trick, the director got the performance he hoped for. In the next take, Cal read the Bible verse as written, but Massey was still furious. In Kazan's words, the film captured "the absolute hatred of Raymond Massey for James Dean, and of James Dean for Raymond Massey."[7]

Another unknown actor, Dick Davalos, was cast as Cal's brother, Aron. Kazan arranged for Dean and Davalos to room together. He hoped to build some genuine brotherly antagonism. Again the director's plan worked. After only a couple of weeks, Davalos grew tired of Dean's unpredictable moods and rudeness.[8] He would be warm and friendly one day, then turn sulky and silent for no apparent reason.

Davalos found working with Dean as challenging as living with him. He never knew exactly what his costar was going to do. Dean seemed to know exactly how to keep other performers on edge. Davalos also realized his costar had problems accepting criticism. "Jimmy had no acting persona that could soak it up and deal with it and not let it get through to him too personally," he said. "It just bewildered him."[9] But Dean listened carefully to Kazan. He did not want to alienate the director who had made superstars of Marlon Brando and Montgomery Clift. Clift had gained recognition for his performances in *A Place in the Sun* and *From Here to Eternity*.

Dean did work well with one member of the cast—Julie Harris. Harris starred as Abra, the young woman both Aron and Cal fell in love with. She remembered Dean fondly, saying: "We were very close. We had a wonderful time working together. . . . He was terrible sensitive with me. I felt we really were doing the parts. That when he looked at me, in the scene, I was Abra to him. I was his brother's girl."[10]

On the Hollywood Set

After the location scenes were wrapped up, filming resumed at the Warner Bros. Studios in Burbank. Most scenes were shot at night. But that did not stop Dean from partying into the wee hours of the morning. He went to bars, smoked marijuana, and drank beer.[11] (Marijuana is an illegal drug that should be avoided.)

Kazan had no intention of letting Dean's socializing distract him from work on the picture. He stepped in and moved his young star into an apartment directly across from his own on the Warner Bros. lot. Now, he could keep an eye on Dean, and he did.

Dean had hoped *Eden* would be his big break. Rumors, "that the kid on the *East of Eden* set was going to make it big," began to fly even before the movie was completed. Kazan recalled the actor's reaction. "The first thing I noticed was that he [Dean] was being rude to our little wardrobe man. I stopped that quickly."[12]

Before *East of Eden* wrapped up, Dean got to meet one of his idols. Marlon Brando was filming nearby. Kazan invited him to stop by the set. A photographer snapped a shot of Kazan, Brando, Harris, and Dean. The picture records Dean's discomfort as he stood in the shadow of the more experienced actor. His body is taut. His mouth clenched. His eyes are not on the camera but focused off in the distance.

"There was so much of Jimmy in that film."

A Wrap

The filming of *East of Eden* finally wrapped up in August, after a dozen weeks of hard work. Dean had done more than give a star-quality performance. In the film, James Dean as Cal Trask gave teenagers a new place in society. For the first time, they were viewed not as oversized children, but as young adults learning to make their own way.

"There was so much of Jimmy in that film," Dean's friend Bill Bast said, ". . . so much of the lost, tormented, searching, gentle, enthusiastic little boy; so much of the bitter, self-abusive, testing, vengeful monster."[13]

On the final day of shooting, Harris went to say good-bye to her young costar. She knocked on the door of Dean's apartment. She had to knock several times before he answered. When he finally opened it, she found him crying, shaking with grief. "It's all over! It's all over!" was all he could say.[14] At that moment, the rebel who wanted to shock and irritate was gone.[15] Another James Dean took center stage—a little lost boy searching for love, for a purpose, and for himself.

Chapter 9

Fame, Fortune, and Romance

On August 9, 1954, after ten weeks of filming, *East of Eden* wrapped up production. The studio gave Dean a weekend to find an apartment. Their policy did not allow actors to "live in" once a movie was completed. Dean had not found a place by Monday, so he came back to the studio expecting to stay longer. Instead, he discovered his luggage and clothes waiting for him at the gate. Before he left, Dean asked William Orr, one of the studio executives, to let him back into his dressing room. Inside Dean reached into a vase and pulled out a wad of bills. "I think it was about $3,500," said Orr.[1]

Dean resented being thrown off the lot.[2] This incident added to his growing hostility toward the studio. He was already unhappy with the Warner Bros. publicity department. They had annoyed him by making up stories about their new young star from Fairmount, Indiana. News releases had portrayed him as an acting genius rescued from life on the farm by director Kazan.

Dean resented these tales and refused to cooperate with the press. When reporters managed to corner him, he defended his actions, saying: "I came here to act, not to please the newspapers."[3]

True Love

Before *East of Eden* reached the movie theaters, Warner Bros. focused on publicity. They wanted to create a glitzy image for James Dean. In Hollywood, the one way for any actor to make news is to date a beautiful young actress. During Dean's time, studios often required stars to go out with one another to attract desirable publicity. Warner Bros. promoted Dean as the dream boyfriend of every girl in America. They paired him with several young starlets, including Pier Angeli. Dean and Angeli's relationship caught the watchful eye of gossip columnists. They reported that Angeli had already discovered Dean, printing this comment attributed to the actress: "James Dean has the lead in *East of Eden* and you'll soon be hearing of him."

Warner Bros. promoted Dean as the dream boyfriend of every girl in America.

Pier's real name was Anna Maria Pierangeli. She lived with her mother and twin sister. The Pierangeli family had recently moved from Italy to Hollywood. Pier's widowed mother was a strict Catholic and had high expectations for her girls. She soon made it clear that James Dean did not meet her standards. She thought her daughter deserved better. After all, Angeli had completed five pictures and earned a salary of one thousand dollars a week.[4] Dean also angered Mrs. Pierangeli with his lack of respect for her Italian ways. Once when she complained that boyfriends in Rome would not bring her daughter home as late as Dean did, he replied, "When in Rome, do as the Romans do. Welcome to Hollywood."[5] He ignored most of Mrs. Pierangeli's complaints, but he did wear a suit when he came to her home.

The young couple's relationship started as a bid for publicity but grew into something stronger. They spent more and more time together. Dean told one reporter, "Pier's a rare girl, I respect her. Unlike most Hollywood girls, she's real and genuine. I can talk to her. She understands."[6]

Pier later recalled special moments with Dean.

> We used to go together to the California coast and stay there secretly in a cottage on a beach far away from prying eyes. We would talk about ourselves and our problems, about the movies and acting, about life and after death. Sometimes we would just go for a walk along the beach, not actually speaking but communicating our love silently to each other. . . . We didn't need to be seen together at film premieres or night clubs. We didn't need to be in gossip columns or be seen at big Hollywood parties.[7]

Angeli and Dean fell in love, though no one approved. Angeli's mother and the studio Angeli worked for thought the two were mismatched. Dean's agent, Jane Deacy, warned him that "if you marry her, you'll be Mr. Pier Angeli."[8] She was telling him that Angeli was

James Dean with girlfriend Pier Angeli in an undated photo.

already a star and that he would be overshadowed by her fame.

Though he cared deeply for Angeli, Dean was confused. When friends asked if he planned to marry her, he told them, "I wouldn't marry her unless I could take care of her properly. And I don't think I'm emotionally stable enough to do so right now."[9]

Dean did promise Angeli that they would work something out. The young couple discussed getting engaged and married, but final plans were postponed. He had to go to New York in August to appear on an episode of the *Philco Television Playhouse*.

Heartbreak

By the time Dean returned to Hollywood, Angeli was engaged to someone else. Singer Vic Damone, a respectable Italian boy, had asked for her hand in marriage. Angeli's mother had given her blessing. Dean was shocked but tried to hide his feelings. He said, "You might say I'm not exactly delighted and happy over her marriage to Vic. . . . I won't try to pretend I'm not sorry—Pier's still OK with me. She broke the news to me the night before she announced her engagement. . . . I hope they'll be happy."[10]

On November 24, 1954, Angeli married Damone. Dean was not on the guest list but made an appearance. Dressed in black leather, he sat on his motorcycle across the street from St. Timothy's Catholic Church. When the newlyweds appeared at the front door, Dean gunned the motorcycle's engine and roared off.

Although Dean wished Angeli happiness, her marriage to Damone lasted only five years. Later, she said she never forgot Dean. "He is the only man I ever loved deeply as a woman should love a man. . . . I don't think one can be in love with one man—even if he is dead—and live with another."[11]

Angeli did see Dean at least one more time a few months after her wedding. Writer Joe Hyams watched her drive away from his house. She was crying. When the writer went inside to see Dean, he was distressed, too. Hyams asked if there was anything he could do. Dean shook his head, saying, "It's already done. Pier's going to have a baby."[12] It was obvious to his friend that Dean thought the baby might be his.

After losing Angeli, Dean went out with several young actresses, including Ursula Andress and Leslie Caron. The studio fixed him up with Terry Moore. The two attended parties and functions when Warner Bros. thought it would be good for publicity.

Dean also experienced the wild side of Hollywood nightlife. His evenings out with friends started at midnight. One of the characters Dean hung out with was an eccentric actress called Vampira, ten years his senior. Dressed in black, she introduced horror movies on TV.

Life After *Eden*

Sneak previews of *East of Eden* were finally released in February 1955. Bill Bast went with a nervous Dean to see the film for the first time. After the showing, Dean knew he had performed well, saying, "Pretty good, wasn't I?"[13]

Critics praised the film. Hedda Hopper even reversed her opinion of the dirty shirt-tailed actor. "I sat spellbound," she commented. "I couldn't remember ever having seen a young man with such power, so many facets of expression, so much sheer invention as this actor."[14]

Another review compared Dean to Brando saying, "He scuffs his feet, he whirls, he pouts, he sputters, he leans against walls, he rolls his eyes, he swallows his words, he ambles slack-kneed—all like Marlon Brando."[15] Dean noted some similarities. They were both from farms, dressed as they pleased, rode motorcycles, and worked for Elia Kazan. Beyond that he did not find the comparison flattering, claiming that "as an actor I have no desire to behave like Brando—and I don't attempt to. I feel within myself there are expressions just as valid and I'll have a few years to develop my own style."[16]

"I couldn't remember ever having seen a young man with such power . . ."

Dean also invited photographer Dennis Stock to attend the preview. "There's no question that a star was born with the first public screening of *East of Eden*," Stock later wrote. "The entire audience applauded loudly as the house lights signaled the end. . . . I knew that I had to do a story on James Dean."[17]

The two met for breakfast the next morning and discussed ideas. They decided that the photo essay should expose the environments that ". . . shaped the unique character of James Byron Dean."[18] Stock sold the photo story to *Life* magazine.

For two weeks, Stock trailed Dean all over Los Angeles, then they went to Indiana. In Fairmount, the photographer captured Dean on the farm, in town, and at the motorcycle shop. One photo showed Dean playing his bongos in a field of pigs and cows. In another, he posed on the driveway of the farmhouse with cousin Markie's dog, Tuck. The actor gazed off in one direction, the dog in the other. Stock captioned that picture, "You can't go home again."

Dean also posed on the stage of his old high school. Though *East of Eden* had not been released, word was out that the movie was going to make James Dean a big Hollywood star. The students treated him like a celebrity, lining up to get his autograph.

Of all the pictures Stock took in Fairmount one became infamous. Dean wanted photos taken at Hunt's, the local funeral parlor. In a back room, the young actor opened a coffin, climbed in, and instructed Stock to snap away. It was a prank the photographer claimed, ". . . but there was a sense of something else." Many claim the photo is evidence that Dean had an unhealthy obsession with death.[19]

In January, Dean and Stock moved on to New York City. They spent another two weeks photographing Dean's old hangouts and checking up on his friends. Stock's photo essay entitled "Moody New Star" was published in *Life* on March 7, 1955. The opening photo showed Dean sitting in his uncle's barn dressed in a suit and tie as he stared at the camera. The closing shot of the young actor was taken in Times Square in New York in the rain. Dean wore a heavy dark raincoat. A cigarette dangled from his mouth, and his face was lost in shadow. He was walking though a large puddle, its surface rippled by tiny drops of rain. Two days after this issue of *Life* hit the newsstands, *East of Eden* was released.

Eden Premiere

East of Eden premiered in New York City. It was a benefit performance with proceeds donated to the Actors Studio. Stars like Marilyn Monroe, Eva Marie Saint, and Marlene Dietrich were celebrity ushers. Jack Warner, Elia Kazan, John Steinbeck, Raymond Massey, and Richard Davalos attended. Dean did not. He returned to Hollywood on March 8—a day before the premiere in New York's Astor Theater.

Dean was overwhelmed by the excitement created by his first film. The center stage spotlight was more exposure than he could handle. He told one friend that having people tell him how good he was embarrassed him. Dean made his excuses to his agent, Deacy, before he left. "I'm sorry, Mom, but you know I can't make this scene. I can't handle it."[20]

His absence was conspicuous at the star-studded benefit for the Actors Studio. People paid $150 for a ticket. They expected to rub elbows with James Dean.

Warner Bros. was furious when their star did not show up. Once again, Dean lived up to his reputation. He ignored the studio's wishes and did just as he pleased. Biographer David Dalton suggested that his rebellious actions sent this message. "It's my party and I'll boycott if I want to."[21]

Reviews of Dean's portrayal of Cal Trask in *East of Eden* were great. Time magazine hailed him as "a young man from Indiana who is unquestionably the biggest news Hollywood has made in 1955."[22] Others called Dean a new kind of talent the film industry badly needed—an actor in touch with his audience.

The director admitted he was completely unprepared for his young star's riotous success.

Kazan was amazed by the reaction of teen fans who screamed for Dean during a Hollywood preview. The director admitted he was completely unprepared for his young star's riotous success.[23]

About this time, Dean's father was interviewed by *Modern Screen*. In the interview, Winton Dean spoke openly about his relationship with his son.

> My Jim is a tough boy to understand. At least he is for me. But maybe that's because I don't understand actors, and he's always wanted to become one. Another reason is that we were separated for a long period of time. From when he was nine until he was eighteen. Those are important, formative years when a boy and his father usually become friends. Jim and I—well, we've never had that closeness. It's nobody's fault, really. Just circumstances . . .[24]

John Steinbeck was the author of the original novel on which *East of Eden* was based. He showed up to the movie's premiere, but James Dean did not.

Dean had reached his goal with the release of his first film. His name was up in lights on theater marquees. He was a star.

Rebel

Financially Dean's future now looked bright. Deacy negotiated a new contract with Warner Bros. He would make nine pictures over the next six years. Though Dean resented the studio's demands and controls over his career, his new contract allowed him to live like a star.

To fill his time while he waited for the studio to pick his next project, Dean decided to pursue a new interest. He started attending local racing events and talked about cars for hours. He finally decided to give racing a try. Dean purchased a white Porsche Speedster convertible and entered the Palm Springs Road Race. At the event, he placed first in the amateur class, and took third when he competed against professionals. One driver who raced against Dean made this comment: "Jimmy wanted his body to hurtle over the ground, the faster the better. . . . His track was the shortest distance from here to there."[25]

In the spring of 1955, the studio called Dean back to work. They had decided on his next project. *Rebel Without a Cause* would be his next movie.

Chapter 10 Rebel

Dean's next movie was actually supposed to be an adaptation of Edna Ferber's novel *Giant*. The cast was ready to roll when a complication delayed the schedule. Elizabeth Taylor, another star in the picture, was pregnant. With the shooting of *Giant* delayed for several months, Warner Bros. gave Dean the green light for a different project, *Rebel Without a Cause*, a low-budget teenage melodrama.

The studio had purchased the rights to *Rebel* in 1946. Dr. Robert Lindner, the book's author, was a prison psychiatrist. The story told the tale of a mentally-disturbed teenager and was set in a prison psychiatric unit. Several writers tried to adapt the book for the screen. Marlon Brando was offered the starring role in 1947, but turned it down, and the project was shelved.

In 1954, director Nicholas Ray created a story he called *The Blind Run*. It focused on juvenile delinquency in Los Angeles. Ray wanted to show that even teens from middle-class backgrounds could turn into juvenile delinquents when parents were preoccupied with their professional and social lives. He felt it was a growing problem that deserved public concern.

Ray also wanted *The Blind Run* to have a romantic theme. "Romeo and Juliet has always struck me as the best play ever written about 'juvenile delinquency,'" he said. "I wanted a Romeo and Juliet feeling about Jim and Judy [the male and female characters]—and their families."[1]

The material for the story came from real life.

Warner Bros. liked his treatment of the timely social issue, but they did not like the title. They took Lindner's title, *Rebel Without a Cause*, and hooked it to Ray's storyline. The movie had no other connection to the plot of Lindner's book.

The Story

Ray's version of *Rebel* is about Jim Stark, the new kid in town. Stark is discontented and rebellious, at odds with his family, friends, and school authorities. His family moved because he got into trouble in the last place they lived. Again, Jim gets off to a bad start as he tries to find the love and acceptance he does not get from his parents. The "gang" at school makes him prove himself in a knife fight and a car race toward the edge of a seaside cliff. The action takes place all in one day as Jim tries to grow up quickly and become a man.

The material for the story came from real life. The director used a pool of information gathered from police, parents, and kids. He did his research in local juvenile homes, police stations, and courtrooms. "The Culver City police liked our approach and offered us everything we needed," Ray said. "Talks with social workers . . . admission to . . . courtrooms, going out on riot calls in a police car."[2]

Irving Shulman, novelist, film writer, and ex-schoolteacher, turned the story line for *Rebel Without a Cause* into a screenplay. He spent about fifteen weeks on the project, then asked to be released from his contract. He did not like working with Ray.[3] Stewart Stern completed the screenplay. When the script was finished, Ray began to select the cast.

The Star and the Director

Ray wanted James Dean to play Jim Stark, the lead role in *Rebel*. He traveled to New York to discuss the project with the young actor. While they talked, he studied Dean's personality and identified traits that could enhance the movie character.

Dean accepted the starring role in *Rebel* and returned to Hollywood. To get into the role, he did his homework during every public appearance. He acted out behaviors displayed by juvenile delinquents. He studied people's reactions, striving for the desired effect. Dean's outrageous behavior made the news. *Parade* magazine reported that he "dressed like an unmade bed; lived in a one-room $30 a month garage apartment; roared to work on a high-powered motorcycle. 'You can sit with Dean all afternoon,' one publicity man told me, 'and he won't open his mouth. He's worse than Brando who at least is articulate.'"[4]

The Cast

Ray had two other important teen roles to fill, Plato and Judy. Natalie Wood tested for Judy. At first Ray did not think she was right for the part. Then one night while casting was still going on, he received a call from Dennis Hopper, who would play a member of the teenage gang in *Rebel*. Dennis and Natalie had been involved in a car accident. Dennis had been drinking, and they had been taken to the police station. Ray went to the station to help them. Natalie had been slightly injured. Her parents came to get her, but she wanted to see Ray first. When he walked into the room, she grabbed him and pulled him down so she could whisper something in his ear. Natalie pointed to the precinct doctor, and said, "He called me a juvenile delinquent. Now do I get the part?"[5]

Ray gave Sal Mineo a shot at the role of Plato. Before making a final decision, the director wanted to see if there was "chemistry" between Dean and Mineo. "I was almost sick. I wanted the part so badly," said Mineo. "We went through a scene and nothing happened between us."[6] Ray suggested the two young men talk for a while. Dean learned that Mineo was from the Bronx. They chatted about life in New York, then moved on to another common interest—cars. The connection was enough. Mineo won the role of Plato.

Nicholas Ray selected Jim Backus as Stark's father.

James Dean and Natalie Wood pose together on the set of *Rebel Without a Cause*.

This was an unusual choice. Backus was a comedian, not a character actor. "It took a great deal of courage on Ray's part to cast me as the father," said Backus. "When we made *Rebel* . . . if the studios needed a henpecked husband, they went into their henpecked husband file—and came up with a little man who fit the image."[7] Ann Doran was cast as Jim's mother, Corey Allen as his rival, and several teens, including Dennis Hopper, who formed "the gang."

A few days before filming began on *Rebel*, Dean disappeared.

Ray encouraged the gang members to hang out together. "Nick's whole thing was to make us a family," said Steffi Sidney, "to make the movie come from us, rather than from his direction. . . . So we all went out together, except for Dean. We went to the beach, climbed around a deserted warehouse one night, to get the feeling of being a group. By the time we were ready to start shooting, we were really thinking as one."[8]

Behind the Scenes

A few days before filming began on *Rebel*, Dean disappeared. "No one knew where he was and Warner's was frantic," Stern said. "Then one morning at about four o'clock my phone rings and I hear 'Mmmmmooooo.' I knew it was Jimmy. . . . How are you, I asked? And Jimmy said he wasn't going to come back. . . . He was gone for ten days and then just showed up one day, ready to work. He never talked about where he had been or why he'd come back."[9] Stern felt certain that something had scared him.

Filming began on March 28, 1955. For four days, the picture was shot in black and white. Then the studio saw how well *East of Eden* was doing at the box office. They decided to film *Rebel* in color.

Ray was delighted. "The first thing I did was pull a red jacket off the Red Cross man, dip it in black paint to take off the sheen and give it to Jimmy."[10] Even today, this jacket remains the image most often associated with the film.

Romance brewed on the set of *Rebel*. Natalie, only sixteen, was having an affair with forty-four-year-old Ray.[11] She was also attracted to Dean and so was Mineo, a closet homosexual. Dean did not return his two costars' interest. At the time, he was involved with Jack Simmons. He even got Simmons a small part in the picture. A homosexual relationship was hinted at in a gossip column item written by Sidney Skolsky, the father of Steffi Sidney, one of Dean's costars in *Rebel Without a Cause*. "Jack is always around the house and set," the columnist wrote. "He gets Jimmy coffee or a sandwich or whatever Jimmy wants. Jack also runs interference for Dean when there are people Jimmy doesn't want to see."[12]

Rumors about the homosexuality of other major stars were making news in 1955 while *Rebel* was in production. It was still considered an immoral activity, and Dean carefully guarded his private affairs. Neither he nor Simmons ever discussed their relationship. It has been "the subject of wild speculation" over the years.[13] Most friends believe that Simmons was devoted to Dean, but that Dean did not return his affection.[14]

The Warner Bros. publicity department worked to create a positive public image for Dean. To play down homosexual rumors, they had starlet Lori Nelson interviewed for a magazine article, "The Dean I've Dated." In the story, Nelson described Dean as "polite, shy, and hesitant, and he stood off, scrutinizing and studying, and saying surprisingly little. . . . [I]t was a pleasant surprise to find him so shy. . . . I went home with a real glow. Everything was so real and honest, and so nice."[15]

The Camera Rolls

James Dean is the first character you see in *Rebel*. He is lying drunk on the sidewalk, curled up next to a toy monkey trying to cover it with a sheet of paper. When the crew was ready to reshoot in color, nothing had been worked out for the opening scene. Dean said, "Please let me do something here; let me play with it. Just roll it."[16]

Bev Long remembered that they had "been working for twenty-three hours straight that day. . . . But we all stayed, as tired as we were, and sat on the curb and watched Dean do that scene. And it was so beautiful that we just *wept*."[17]

Dennis Hopper, one of the gang members, remembered Dean's interpretation of the arrest scene. "When the police find him and search him, this angry drunk guy is suddenly ticklish. Where did that come from? . . . Nobody directed him to do that. James Dean directed James Dean."[18] His sense of timing created unexpected moments that gave *Rebel* lasting impact.

Ray encouraged the teenage cast to improvise and suggest changes in scenes. In one "rumble" scene, the director had all the kids running down the alley, shouting and carrying on. Beverly Long said, "We told him it just wasn't done like that. When gangs rumbled, they didn't invite twelve hundred people. They did it . . . quietly, otherwise the authorities would come."[19]

Filming continued into May. Some emotionally charged scenes had to be shot over and over. The cameras rolled only when Dean worked himself up and into character. He kept the cast and crew waiting an hour before the long scene at the opening of the movie. The scene introduced the three main characters as they are each hauled into juvenile hall for different offenses. To capture the appropriate mood, Dean sat alone in his dressing room guzzling wine and listening to Wagner's "Ride of the Valkyries."[20]

He kept the cast and crew waiting an hour before the long scene at the opening of the movie.

Dean disrupted the schedule twice while *Rebel* was being filmed. The first time was due to illness. He contracted malaria and was in bed for several days. He took off another day to enter an auto race in Bakersfield. Otherwise, he was front and center daily, ready to work.

In spite of Kazan's warnings regarding Dean's wild habits, Ray developed a good relationship with his star. The director even rehearsed scenes from the movie in the living room of his own home with him. Ray portrayed Jim Stark's father and helped his young star get into character. The director realized that "for a successful collaboration . . . [h]e [Dean] needed reassurance, tolerance, [and] understanding. An important way of creating this was to involve him at every stage in the development of the picture."[21]

"James Dean worked very closely with Nick," Jim Backus later said in *Variety*. "May I say that this is the first time in the history of motion pictures that a twenty-four-year-old boy, with only one movie to his credit, was practically the co-director. Dean insisted on utter realism, and, looking back, I sometimes wonder how we finished so violent a picture without someone getting seriously injured."[22]

During the knife fight outside the planetarium, Dean and Corey used real switchblades.

During the knife fight outside the planetarium, Dean and Corey used real switchblades. They wore chest protectors under their shirts, but still they could have been seriously hurt. Ray once cut the action as the scene was being filmed when he saw a trickle of blood running down Dean's neck. Dean was irate, saying, "What the hell are you doing? Can't you see I'm having a real moment? Don't you ever cut a scene while I'm having a real moment."[23]

Near the end of production, Dean talked about his future as a director. *The Little Prince* was a project he dreamed of tackling.

It's a Wrap

The production of *Rebel Without a Cause* wrapped up on May 26, 1955. Dean and Ray knew the movie was something special. The director remembered their last moments on the set. "Jimmy and I were left alone. . . . Everyone but the gateman had gone home. We were wandering around under the lights making sure we hadn't left anything behind. We really didn't want to admit it was all over. I said, 'Let's go. We've nothing more to do here.'"[24]

The experience also left other members of the cast with great memories. Natalie Wood remembered working with Dean:

> He was so inspiring, always so patient and kind. He didn't act as though he were a star at all. . . . He was great when he played a scene, he had the ability to make everyone else look great, too. He used to come on the set and watch the scenes, even when he wasn't in them. He was interested in the whole picture and not just his part.[25]

During a 1974 television special devoted to James Dean, Peter Lawford interviewed Sal Mineo. The two were standing near the planetarium used in *Rebel* scenes. Mineo said, "This place is full of spirits for me. Not only Jimmy's spirit but my spirit and everyone involved in that picture because it was an incredible experience. . . .

It wasn't just making a movie. It was as close to a spiritual experience as you can get. It all happened because of him."[26]

James Dean appeared in almost every scene of *Rebel Without a Cause*. He delivered a performance that many never forgot, and he became a role model for the troubled middle-class teenager.

Chapter 11

Giant

Rebel wrapped up on May 26, 1955. Dean reported immediately to wardrobe and makeup for his next film, *Giant*. Edna Ferber's novel was expected to be the blockbuster of the year. The best-selling book permitted its author to negotiate a great deal for the movie rights. Any studio who wanted the novel had to include Ferber as one of the picture's producers. Warner Bros. finally worked out an agreement with her.

George Stevens was selected to direct the film, and he started work on the project in 1953. Dean was filming *East of Eden* when he learned that the director and scriptwriter were holed up in an office near his dressing room. He approached the director, saying "Hey, Mr. Stevens, that part of Jett Rink in *Giant*—that's for me."[1]

Stevens was not sure about that. In his opinion, Dean's personality, size, and style did not fit the part of Rink, a poor Texas ranch hand who strikes oil and transforms himself into a flashy millionaire playboy. However, after Alan Ladd rejected the role, Stevens gave Dean a shot.

The movie, based on Edna Ferber's best-selling novel, shows how the discovery of oil affected the economy of Texas. The story begins when rancher Bick Benedict visits a Maryland farm to buy a horse and meets the owner's daughter, Leslie. They fall in love, marry, and return to his Texas ranch. As the couple settle down and raise a family, oil is discovered on land all around them. At first, Benedict refuses to drill for oil and continues to raise cattle as he always has. The story, spanning two generations, focuses on Benedict's never-ending feud with Jett Rink.

Dean entered his white Porsche 356 Super Speedster in the road race.

Stevens lined up an impressive cast for *Giant*. Elizabeth Taylor, James Dean, Rock Hudson, Mercedes McCambridge, Chill Wills, Carroll Baker, Sal Mineo, Earl Holliman, Dennis Hopper, and Jane Withers were the picture's headliners.

Before Dean had to report to location to begin work on *Giant*, he had three days off. He decided to go to Santa Barbara for the Memorial Day weekend. Stevens had banned him from racing while *Giant* was in production, so this was his last chance to pursue his passion for a while. Dean entered his white Porsche 356 Super Speedster in the road race. He drove hard and fast, hoping to win, but his luck did not hold. During the last lap the Porsche blew a piston and he had to drop out.

On Location in Texas

On June 3, Dean joined *Giant*'s cast. He was still exhausted from work on *Rebel* and under a doctor's orders to eat a high protein diet. Though time was limited, Dean had already done his homework for his role as Jett Rink. He had boned up on Texas history and cattle ranching. He showed up wearing Levi's, cowboy boots, and a ten-gallon hat.

Marfa, Texas, was a three-and-a-half-hour drive from El Paso, and about sixty miles north of the Mexican border. The town was in the middle of the desert and had little to offer in the way of nightlife. There were a couple of bars and one movie theater, which the *Giant* company used to screen the film that they shot each day. Less than three thousand people lived in and around the community. The picture's stars stayed in homes rented from locals.

A Hollywood movie company was a novelty in Marfa. Every day, crowds numbering almost a thousand would show up to watch the company film. Hot daytime temperatures, usually above one hundred degrees, did not keep spectators away. The locals were used to the heat, but the cast and crew found it unbearable. No homes in Marfa had air-conditioning in 1955.

Much of the filming took place on two large ranches nearby. The exterior of a huge Victorian house was built on one location. It was a three-sided structure with a hollow interior and could be seen from miles away across the flat, dusty Texas landscape.

In Character

Dean breathed real life into the screen image of Jett Rink. He moved as if riding a horse was something he had done everyday of his life. His cowboy hat was simply another part of his body. His skin appeared weathered by daily exposure to the harsh Texas sun and wind. By the beginning of July, Dean had also perfected a Texas accent and had taught himself to rope steers.

"Jimmy was a dedicated perfectionist . . . ," wrote Mercedes McCambridge. "He asked cowboys to teach him intricate tricks with a rope. He worked himself bleary-eyed with that rope, but if you watch him as Jett Rink doing tricks with it, you will see a Texas boy who has been working with a rope all his cotton-pickin' life."[2]

Another actor in *Giant*, Joe Brown, had known Dean in theater arts at UCLA. He was impressed with the way Dean got ready for each scene.

> There's one thing that remained with him from the days at UCLA. Before he'd go on stage, he wouldn't be like some of the other cats who'd be playing around; he'd get quiet and then *go on!* He did the same thing on *Giant*. I'd hang around and watch him shoot and I noticed his concentration, that *tremendous concentration*. I mean he'd be so absorbed in a scene that a gun could have gone off and he wouldn't have heard it. . . . And I think a

On the set of *Giant*, James Dean gets a lesson on how to use a lasso.

> lot of people misinterpreted that, thinking him kind of snobbish, but an actor has to do that.[3]

Author Edna Ferber visited the set in Texas. She liked Dean and was delighted by his eagerness to know her vision for Jett's personality. "I don't think there is another actor in the world who can convey Jett as well as he did,"[4] she said.

Stormy Weather on Location

From the first day on location, the young actor had problems working with George Stevens. The director made unreasonable demands, in Dean's opinion. Stevens wanted all the cast in makeup at all times, even if they were not needed for any of the scenes scheduled. That way, if changes had to be made to the schedule for some reason, everyone was ready without delay. But it was exhausting to hang around in the hot, dusty Texas weather. After standing by for three days in a row, Dean did not show up on the fourth day. Stevens got mad and he yelled at him in front of the cast and crew.

"I don't think there is another actor in the world who can convey Jett as well as he did,"

The reprimand made Dean sulk and pout. He turned to the two cast members he got along with, Taylor and McCambridge, for support and comfort.

For Stevens, the creativity of moviemaking happened in the cutting room. He used more than six hundred thousand feet of film for *Giant*. It took a year to edit down to its final movie version, more than three hours in length. Dean nicknamed Stevens the "round-the-clock director" because of his technique and complained to his friend Bill Bast. "The more Jimmy became aware of the mechanics of Stevens'[s] approach," wrote Bast, "the more he began to resent the man. Stevens shot scenes from every conceivable angle then spent months editing out the excess footage."[5]

Dean also had quirks that annoyed the director. He made Stevens's editing job more difficult because he would not deliver the same performance twice during retakes of scenes. Stevens also refused to let Dean add any spontaneous interpretations to his character's part. He insisted he stick to the script as it was written.

Dean worked well with Taylor and McCambridge but clashed with Rock Hudson. "I didn't like him particularly," Hudson said later:

> He and I and Chill Wills lived in a rented house together for three months while we were . . . in Texas and . . . Dean was hard to be around. He hated George Stevens, didn't think he was a good director, and he was always angry and full of contempt. He never smiled. He was sulky and he had no manners. . . . And he was rough to do a scene with. . . . While doing a scene, in the giving and taking, he was just a taker. He would suck everything out and never give back.[6]

Dean spent most of his free time with dialogue coach Bob Hinkle. At night, the two would go rabbit hunting. In the five weeks they filmed in Texas, they bagged a total of two hundred sixty-one rabbits, plus two coyotes. Hinkle also showed him rope tricks, teaching him how to build a loop with the rope. Dean mastered that trick before the crew returned to Hollywood.

Residents of Marfa liked Dean, and he later said, "I've gotten to like the state and the people so much I'm apt to talk like a proud Texan even after *Giant* is complete."[7] Lucy Garcia, then a Marfa teenager, remembered that Hudson and Taylor never mingled with the townsfolk. Dean, however, talked to them, signing autographs willingly.[8]

His interaction with the locals was partly homework. It allowed him to study their accent and to mimic mannerisms, especially the unique gait of cowboys who had spent their lives in the saddle.

Back in Hollywood

Giant's cast and crew returned to Los Angeles near the end of July and went to work on the studio's soundstage. Dean settled quickly into his old ways—enjoying Hollywood nightlife to its fullest. His regular companion was actress Ursula Andress.

Stevens continued to demand that the cast be available at all times. He and Dean locked horns regularly over this issue. After being out half the night, the young actor hated getting up at dawn to report to the studio for several hours of costume and makeup. It upset him even more to get on the set at eight sharp and find he was not needed until late morning or afternoon. Actors usually played cards, read, smoked cigarettes, drank coffee, and talked as they waited to be called. This did not work for Dean. Distractions destroyed the concentration he needed to give his best performance. Dean showed his displeasure for being kept waiting by arriving late most mornings.[9] Then, one Saturday he did not show up at all. He had taken the day off to move into a house he had rented. When Stevens found out he blew up. He did not need the actor for any scenes but wanted him present and accounted for. Stevens also vowed never to work with Dean again.[10]

The next day Stevens raked Dean over the coals and threatened to see that he never worked on another Hollywood film. Dean replied to his tirade, "Let me tell *you* something. I am not a machine. I prepared *all night* for that scene. I came in ready to work and you kept me sitting around all day. . . . And you're *not* going to stop me from working."[11] Hollywood columnists reported this bit of gossip, gloating a bit over the jam Dean got himself into.

A Star Again

Even with all this trouble, word during the final weeks of shooting was that Dean was exceptional in *Rebel Without a Cause* and maybe even better in *Giant*.

His agent, Deacy, approached Warner Bros. to negotiate a new contract. She made demands. The most important was that Dean wanted to establish his own production company at Warner's. Projects he hoped to pursue included *The Little Prince* and *The Story of Billy the Kid*.

The studio had already lined up Dean's next project. It was to be a screen biography of the boxer, Rocky

Graziano, called *Somebody Up There Likes Me*. Pier Angeli would play the part of Graziano's wife. The young actor was already preparing for the role, training with a professional boxer.

At twenty-four, James Dean had achieved his dream. He was a Hollywood star with a bright future ahead of him.

Chapter 12

The Last Race

By the middle of September 1955, the production of *Giant* had almost wrapped up, but Dean needed to reshoot a few scenes before his work was finished. During that time, he also made a public-service announcement for the National Safety Council. The black-and-white commercial was a short interview with him by actor Gig Young. Dean wore cowboy attire and brought a favorite prop from *Giant*, the rope and the rock he used for a lasso trick. When the camera rolled, Dean went into his act, twirling his rope as he replied to questions about driving too fast. He admitted that he took a lot of unnecessary chances on the highway and said, "You don't know what this guy is going to do—or the other one. On a track there are a lot of men who spend a lot of time developing rules and ways of safety. I find myself being cautious on the highway. I don't have the urge to speed. . ."[1] As he was about to leave, Young asked if he had any special advice for the young drivers.

Dean looked straight at the camera and pointed to himself with one thumb. "Take it easy driving," he said. "The life you might save might be mine."[2] With that he walked quickly off stage, and Young closed the door behind him.

A Spyder for Dean

With his work on *Giant* finally completed, Dean had time to pursue other interests. He purchased a new sports car and entered a race at the end of September. The lightweight Porsche Spyder 550 could hit speeds of one hundred twenty or better.

On the night he bought it, Dean drove to one of his favorite restaurants, the Villa Capri. He wanted to show off his new purchase to friend, Patsy D'Amore, the restaurant's owner. He also showed his new car to one of the guests, British actor Alec Guinness. Guinness later recalled his reaction. "I heard myself saying in a voice I could hardly recognize as my own 'Please, never get in it.'"[3]

A couple of days later, Dean took his car back to the dealer to be customized. His racing number, 130, was painted on the hood, the trunk, and both doors.

Off to the Races

On the morning of September 30, 1955, Dean woke early, dressed in blue slacks, a white T-shirt, a red windbreaker, and sunglasses. He packed his Ford station wagon for the trip to Salinas where the races were to take place the next day. He locked up the house and drove to the dealership to pick up his car.

Rolf Weutherich, the mechanic, was working on the Spyder, getting it race-ready. He planned to ride along in case the car needed fine tuning. Dean had also invited two other friends, stuntman Bill Hickman and Sandy Roth. Roth, a photographer, was shooting a photo-essay for *Collier's* magazine featuring Dean.

At ten o'clock, his father, Winton, and his Uncle Charles Nolan stopped at the car dealer to check out Dean's new toy. Dean tried to talk his uncle into going to the race, but Nolan had other plans. This was also the last day Marcus and Ortense Winslow would be in Los Angeles. It was the end of their month-long visit with Winton Dean. They were driving back to Indiana. After saying good-bye to his father and uncle, Dean and his friends discussed how they would get to Salinas.

Dean decided to drive the Porsche. Weutherich rode with him. Sandy and Bill followed in the station wagon. They pulled a trailer that the Porsche could be loaded on. The four set out about one thirty in the afternoon and headed north from Los Angeles on Route 99. Dean set the pace, with the station wagon trailing close behind. Weutherich said, "I'd never seen Jimmy so happy. He talked and laughed and seemed very at ease."[4]

A few miles south of Bakersfield, Dean hit a downhill grade and got the Porsche up to sixty-five miles an hour. California Highway Patrol Officer Otie V. Hunter pulled

James Dean gasses up his Porsche Spyder on the morning of the day he died. This is possibly the last photo of him alive.

him over. The officer gave him a ticket, even though Dean tried to talk his way out of the violation. He knew the press would turn this minor violation into headline news, especially since only two weeks earlier he had made the commercial warning teenagers about driving too fast on the highway.

It was late afternoon when Dean turned off Route 99 onto 466. He picked up speed as he drove west. He wanted to reach Salinas as soon as possible, so he could get a good night's rest before the race the next day. They made one more stop at a gas station near Routes 466 and 33. The sun was going down, but Dean did not turn on his headlights as he drove off.

After several miles, the road began to twist and turn as it climbed some foothills. Dean passed several cars. Once he badly misjudged the distance between himself and the oncoming car, nearly causing a head-on collision. The other vehicle pulled off on the shoulder at the last moment, preventing an accident. Dean and Weutherich raced on through the dusky light toward the intersection of Route 466 and 41.

The Accident

As he sped along, Dean spotted a black-and-white Ford sedan. Its driver was getting ready to turn left off Route 466 onto 41. To do this, the Ford would have to cross Dean's lane. "That guy up there's gotta stop," he said to Weutherich, "He'll see us."[5] Even as he spoke, the Ford began to turn. As it made the maneuver, it ended up facing the Porsche head-on, and then slowed down for no apparent reason. This happened so quickly, Dean had little time to respond. Instead of hitting the brakes, he decided to floor it, hoping he could speed up and swerve around the larger car. This was a technique well-trained sports car drivers used to avoid wrecks on the track. Unfortunately, there was not enough room for Dean to miss the Ford. The driver's side of the Spyder slammed into the driver's side of the Ford. People nearby reported that the crash sounded like a bomb had exploded. The Ford slid to a stop on the highway. Its driver sat slumped behind the wheel momentarily, but was able to walk away from the car.

Dean's Porsche careened off the road and rolled to a halt near a telephone pole. Weutherich was thrown from the car into a field about fifteen feet away. Dean was trapped in the wreckage of the Spyder. His feet were stuck between the clutch and the brake pedals, his body slung across the passenger seat. Other cars stopped to help. One driver hurried off to find the nearest phone to call the police and an ambulance.

At the Scene

The police and ambulance had arrived when Roth and Hickman pulled up in the station wagon. Roth described the scene on that September afternoon. "I noticed what seemed like some kind of roadblock. . . ," Roth said.

> As I came closer, the obstruction took form. It was a sedan, not badly damaged in the middle of the highway. . . . Off in a ditch to the right, I suddenly saw what had been the sleek, silver Porsche—now

> it was like a crumpled pack of cigarettes. Rolf had been thrown clear of the car: Jim was dead in his seat. The impact had thrown his head back too far.[6]

The ambulance driver pulled Dean from the mangled car, and Hickman held him while the paramedics brought the gurney. Roth stood back from the wreck and snapped photographs. Even at the moment of death, Dean was captured on film.

The ambulance took Dean and Weutherich to War Memorial Hospital in Paso Robles. Hickman followed behind in the Ford. At the hospital, Dr. Robert Bossert pronounced Dean dead before his body was removed from the ambulance.

An official death certificate was issued on October 3, 1955. Paul Merrick, the county coroner, stated that death was caused by a broken neck. The time of death was set at 5:45 P.M. Merrick also stated that the accident took place one mile east of Cholame at the junction of Route 466 and 41.

Doctors in the hospital worked frantically on Weutherich. He had numerous cuts and broken bones. One leg was so badly fractured doctors were not sure they could save it. Weutherich made a complete recovery, but he spent a year in the hospital while the leg and other broken bones healed.

Investigation

At the accident site the California Highway Patrol tried to sort out what had happened. They interviewed the driver of the Ford, twenty-three year old Donald

Turnupseed. A veteran of the navy, he was now a freshman at California Polytechnic Institute. Turnupseed had been on his way home for the weekend. He had suffered only a few cuts and bruises, but was in a state of shock. He kept saying over and over, "I didn't see him."[7]

Because Dean died in the accident an inquest was held. Turnupseed testified that he did not see the Spyder until it was too late to avoid a collision. Though Dean did not have his lights on and was driving too fast in the dusky light, the verdict concluded it was an accident. Neither Dean nor Turnupseed were found to be at fault.

After the accident, Turnupseed refused all interviews until a few months before his death in 1995. Then he spoke with a California radio presenter, Maria Moretti. He told her he had lied at the time of the accident. He had seen the Spyder, but he was distracted by a Kay Starr and Doris Day program on the car radio.[8] Lack of concentration had caused him to misjudge Dean's speed and the distance between the two cars. Turnupseed kept silent all these years because of hate mail and even physical attacks from Dean fans.

Headline News

After Dean was pronounced dead, a hospital operator telephoned Warner Bros. Studios. A night watchman took the message and passed the news on to Henry Ginsberg, *Giant*'s producer. Ginsberg called Dick Clayton, Dean's representative in Hollywood. Clayton called Jane Deacy. She had just checked into a hotel in Los Angeles. Negotiations for a new contract for Dean were planned for the next week. Clayton then drove to Winton Dean's home to break the news of his son's death.

Ginsberg also called George Stevens. Stevens and several actors were in a screening room watching a rough cut of *Giant*. After he took the call, Stevens stopped the film and turned on the lights. Everyone turned to look at him. He relayed the terrible news to the others. There had been a car crash and James Dean was dead.

Elizabeth Taylor was in the room. "There was an intake of breath," she wrote later. "No one said anything. I couldn't believe it; none of us could."[9] Taylor was too upset to work the next day. She was eventually hospitalized to recover from an emotional breakdown caused by Dean's death.

Elizabeth Taylor was eventually hospitalized to recover from an emotional breakdown caused by Dean's death.

The news aired in Hollywood on Friday evening. By Sunday, papers across the United States and around the world published reports of the accident and obituaries. The coverage of Dean's death was exceptional considering only one of his three movies had been released.

The next morning, Saturday, October 1, 1955, the banner headline of the *Marion Leader-Tribune* in Indiana read: "James Dean Is Killed in Automobile Wreck."

The subtitle added more details: "Fairmount Man Died in Traffic Accident in West."[10] That was how most Fairmount citizens learned of his death.

Final Resting Place

Two people who loved Dean most did not hear the news on Friday night or even on Saturday. Marcus and Ortense Winslow had set out for Indiana as planned at around the same time Dean headed for Salinas. When the accident took place, the Winslows were on the road. As they were driving, Marcus heard a radio newscaster announce that a young actor had been killed. Ortense was sleeping at the time, and Marcus turned the car radio off before the name was revealed. He had a feeling the news was about his nephew. If it was, he did not want to know until he was home.[11]

When Marcus and Ortense reached Fairmount on Monday evening, their daughter, Joan, met them. She told them the sad news. Marcus called Winton in Los Angeles. Winton had planned to bury Dean next to his mother in the cemetery in Marion. Marcus wanted him laid to rest in Fairmount's Park Cemetery. Winton agreed.

Four days after the accident, Winton brought his son's body back to Hunt's Funeral Parlor in Fairmount, Indiana. The memorial service was held on Saturday, October 8, 1955, at the Fairmount Friends Church. Reverends James De Weerd and Xen Harvey presided. Dean's body rested at the front of the church in a closed coffin, covered with flowers. The organ played "Going

Home" from Dvorak's New World Symphony. Six hundred people packed the tiny Fairmount church. Twenty-four hundred more gathered outside, listening to the service over a loudspeaker.

Harvey's eulogy titled, "The Life of James Dean: A Drama in Three Acts," ended with these words: "The career of James Dean has not ended. It has just begun . . . God himself is directing the production."[12]

De Weerd focused on the content of Dean's short life, saying that "he accomplished more than most persons do if they live to be seventy or eighty."[13]

Dennis Stock, the photographer who had taken the *Life* magazine photos of Dean, was one of the mourners who had flown in from California. He never forgot Marcus Winslow's distress. "It was as though he was in a state of shock," he said, "almost incapable of taking in the fact of Dean's death."[14] Stock offered his support and stood by Marcus during the graveside ceremony at Park Cemetery.

James Byron Dean was buried in the Park Cemetery in Fairmount, Indiana, on October 8, 1955. A simple granite tombstone marks his final resting place, just a few miles south of the Indiana farm he called home.

Chapter 13 Dean Mania

Before James Dean drove off into the twilight in his silver-gray Spyder 550, many recognized the young actor's potential. But he had not attained the sensational fame of a Hollywood *giant*. That made reaction to his death all the more astonishing. The breaking news was wired to papers across the country and around the world. Headlines frequently announced the story in bold print on the top of page one. Even publications such as *The New York Times*, *Newsweek*, and *Time* magazines that rarely ran copy about little-known actors printed Dean's obituary. These notices were brief, listing only the basic facts. However, they seemed to confirm the importance of this rising young star.

Rebel

On October 3, 1955, *Rebel Without a Cause* opened, and teenagers lined up to see the new James Dean movie. Some saw it twenty or thirty times. Young fans identified and wept with Jim Stark. They also wept for the young actor, their new idol, lost before they had time to know him. A whole new cult grew around the star of *Rebel*, and Warner Bros. knew they had a smash hit. Everywhere teenagers mimicked Dean. They wore blue jeans and red windbreakers. They slouched as they walked and styled their hair like his.

Reviewers applauded the movie. "Extraordinary [sic] good acting by the late James Dean, Natalie Wood, and Sal Mineo,"[1] said Jack Moffitt in the *Hollywood Reporter*. *Daily Variety* noted how Dean had matured. The Brando mannerisms observed in *East of Eden* were gone. He was developing a distinctive style all his own. Dean collected several honors for *Rebel*. The Hollywood Foreign Press awarded him a Golden Globe. *Modern Screen* gave him a Silver Cup for Special Achievement.

Everywhere teenagers mimicked Dean.

Then, in February 1956, the Academy of Motion Picture Arts and Sciences nominated Dean for an Oscar for his portrayal of Cal Trask in *East of Eden*. When Ernest Borgnine was named best actor instead, many fans, including Hedda Hopper, were angered.[2] Hopper vented in her column, demanding that the academy give Dean an honorary Oscar the following year.

Devastated Fans

In the weeks following his death, James Dean's popularity grew. His fans planted the seeds for his legend. In New York and Los Angeles, they ransacked places he had called home. Fans needed something they could touch to help them remember the fallen star. As many as five hundred showed up daily to view his grave. Others sent flowers, so many that Fairmount florists struggled to keep up with the orders.

That fall, several hundred letters a week arrived at the Warner Bros. Studios addressed to Dean. By January 1956, the number grew to more than three thousand a month, and in July the studio received seven thousand letters for him. Now Dean's fans were newsworthy.

Newsweek ran a feature titled "Star That Won't Die." The article described the flood of mail logged in at the studios addressed to James Dean. "Many Dean fans even refused to believe he is dead," *Newsweek* reported, "Dean, according to this gospel, was only mutilated in the smashup, but so badly that he is being kept out of sight in a hospital, against his will."[3]

Fans also called television stations. They wanted old programs aired in which he appeared. They scoured stores for photographs of Dean, purchased busts of him in stone or cast in bronze. Others formed clubs to help keep his memory alive.

On Sunday, October 6, 1956, a ceremony marking the first anniversary of Dean's death was held at Park Cemetery in Fairmount. Reverend James De Weerd placed a wreath on the grave. It was a gift from Dean's fans in West Germany. "We are grateful . . . ," De Weerd told the crowd of two thousand, "James Dean, one of our young men, has earned world acclaim in his chosen field of dramatic arts. On behalf of the James Dean fans of West Germany, we place this wreath in his honor, on this, the first anniversary of his untimely death."[4]

The Legend Grows

The world premiere of *Giant* took place a few days later. It opened in New York on October 10 and in Los Angeles on October 18. Then in February 1957, James Dean was nominated for his second Academy Award. This time he seemed to stand a good chance to win for his portrayal of Jett Rink. But Warner Bros. erred. They placed Dean in the category of best actor instead of the best supporting actor. That year, the award was claimed by Yul Brynner for the musical, *The King and I*.

Though *Giant* was his third and final film, the James Dean legend did not fade. He was now an American idol known around the world. During the fifties and sixties, his fame spread to England, France, Germany, Holland, Italy, Spain, Sweden, Finland, and Japan. By the 1980s, James Dean, Elvis Presley, and Marilyn Monroe were the three best-known American movie stars. All kinds of objects featuring Dean were produced and sold: miniature busts, key rings, mugs, glasses, buttons, pins, masks, T-shirts, red rebel windbreakers, posters, calendars, pencils, lighters, plates, ashtrays, postcards, pillowcases, sunglasses, and much more. Many companies used his image to sell their products. The face and name of James Dean attracted attention even beyond the grave.

Graveyard Antics

Over the years, fans continue to visit Dean's grave. They come to take pictures or just to look at it. Women kiss the gravestone, leaving lipstick prints behind. Other fans leave notes or packs of cigarettes.

The Fairmount police have recorded strange antics at his grave site in Park Cemetery. In 1980, they found a teenage boy trying to sleep on the grave. One night in 1991, Officer Carl Adams discovered a couple who were getting ready to make love on the grave. On what would have been Dean's fifty-fifth birthday, a local journalist found a fifteen-year-old fan sitting on a rock in front of his grave. She was reading aloud "A Country Pathway" by James Whitcomb Riley. The poet was one of Dean's favorite writers.

On April 12, 1983, the cemetery groundskeeper noticed that Dean's tombstone was gone. He reported the theft to the police. It was spotted that same day along a county road and returned. Three weeks later, it disappeared again. This time, months passed before it turned up. A firefighter in Fort Wayne, Indiana, discovered it. The stone was resting near a dumpster behind his fire station. Marcus Winslow, Jr., picked it up that afternoon and took it back to Fairmount. The thief later explained his action in a letter to a Fort Wayne newspaper. "You have heroes," said the man, remaining anonymous,

> How would you like to see their grave messed up? What would you think if you . . . saw people had

> spray painted their names all over . . . had chipped stone away. . . . We'd rather take it away entirely than have it die a terrible death. . . . I just wanted the family to know I didn't mean to hurt anyone, and I did it out of admiration and the fact that the tombstone was going to hell. A lot of us consider Dean to be one of the finest actors who ever lived.[5]

Straight or Gay?

Over the years, questions about Dean's sexuality have persisted. He had many male friends, both straight and gay, and some claim Dean was homosexual. One close friend, Martin Landau, disputes this myth, saying that "when we [Dean and Landau] were together, we were two guys . . . looking at girls, hitting on girls."[6]

At twenty-four, Dean was still a kid who needed to grow up. Like other young men, he needed to experiment with many relationships before settling down with a true love. It is fairly certain that a brief homosexual encounter between Dean and Rogers Brackett did occur. But he also had several serious heterosexual relationships with Dizzy Sheridan, Pier Angeli, and Barbara Glenn.

As an actor, Dean felt the need to experiment, to soak up different experiences in all aspects of life. With each acting role, he had to become someone else. The more he understood human nature the easier it was to portray characters realistically. Dean studied people and sexual relationships like any lesson that needed to be mastered.[7]

Legacy

As the years passed, sociologists attempted to explain Dean's lasting appeal. They pointed to the parallel between his brief life, those of his movie characters, and what had happened in American society. Beginning in the fifties, teenagers gained new status. Before that time, teens were looked on as big "kids." They had little power and no heroes of their own. Dean became one of the first teen role models. He acted out their rage, rebellion, loneliness, and confusion—common emotions teens experienced but were not supposed to express.

He acted out their rage, rebellion, loneliness, and confusion.

In the sixties he stood for rebelliousness and discontent. Radicals identified with him. Many believe Dean inspired the movie *Easy Rider* with its fact-filled commentary on America in the sixties. Dennis Hopper, the picture's director, admits that he had a great admiration for Dean.

In the seventies, The Eagles rock band recorded the song "James Dean" for their first album. The Fairmount Historical Museum opened, featuring a display of Dean memorabilia. In 1977, Seita Ohnishi, a wealthy Japanese businessman, built a memorial to Dean in Cholame, in front of the town's post office.

In 1990, on the thirty-fifth anniversary of Dean's death, thirty thousand people came to Fairmount to the surprise of many, including Ortense Winslow.

"We've had kids come from France, from Japan, from all over America," she said. "They've seen his movies on television and say they had to come. I've burned thousands of letters and I've got thousands left. I just wish somebody would tell me what it's all about."[8]

During the first couple of years after Dean's death, many young actors tried to imitate his style. Casting directors quickly grew tired of the copycats. Eventually, Dean did inspire many actors who followed him—to be themselves and give their best. These actors stood out from the rest, refusing to be anything other than themselves. Steve McQueen, Jack Nicholson, Clint Eastwood, Martin Sheen, Robert DeNiro, Nicolas Cage, Sean Penn, and Johnny Depp are sometimes compared with James Dean because they, too, followed their own dreams.

Cage said, "I became an actor when I saw James Dean in *East of Eden*. It was the breakdown scene with his father. It was so emotional and heartbreaking that I knew right then and there what I wanted to do. I wanted to act."[9] When Cage won his Academy Award for *Leaving Las Vegas* (1995), he made a point of putting James Dean first on his list of people to thank.

Martin Sheen also admired Dean. "When I was in acting school in New York years ago, there was a saying that if Marlon Brando changed the way people acted, then James Dean changed the way people lived. He was the greatest actor who ever lived. He was simply a genius."[10]

James Dean Country Today

When visitors make a trip to rural Indiana where James Dean grew up, they get a taste of what life was like in the forties. Fairmount looks much the same as it did when he was living there. A first stop for fans was the James Dean Gallery, located on Interstate 69 near Gas City, Indiana. The museum opened its new facility on May 15, 2004. It housed the world's largest James Dean exhibit. It featured displays that explored his childhood, rise to stardom, and his tragic death. Visitors could also watch a video that included rare television appearances and early screen tests made by Dean. The gallery closed in February 2006. The James Dean exhibit is now on display at the WWII Victory Museum in Auburn, Indiana.

From Interstate 69, it is a short drive to Fairmount. A tourist map provides directions to places important to fans: the Winslow Farm, Carter's motorcycle shop, and Dean's grave. After touring sites, visitors will want to stop at the Fairmount Historical Museum. There they can see Dean's first motorcycle, some of his original paintings, and photographs from the family's collection. Many of the locals manning the museum knew Dean when he lived in Indiana. They gladly walk guests through the rooms, pointing out objects of special interest, and telling tales of the good old days when Dean was a teenager—stories not found in biographies about him.

At the end of September, the museum sponsors

their annual "Remembering James Dean Festival." This event features a Grand Parade, a James Dean Look-Alike Contest, the James Dean Run, a pre-1970 car show, the James Dean Rock-Lasso Contest, and screenings of his movies.

Forever Young

Even now, more than fifty years after his accident, the face of James Dean is still recognized around the world. Many remember his brief life, and in June 2005, they celebrated the fiftieth anniversary of his death at the James Dean Fest held in Marion, Indiana. The theme selected for this anniversary was a quote from Dean and certainly reflected his life, "Dream as if you'll live forever. Live as if you'll die today."[11]

Fans that came to celebrate the life of the star who remained forever young, were rewarded with a special treat. They witnessed the American preview of a new ninety-minute documentary about James Byron Dean. They also heard the entertaining tale of how this film, *James Dean: Forever Young*, fulfilled a lifetime dream for Mike Sheridan, the writer, producer, and director. The story began in 1956. Sheridan was a sixteen-year-old fan. He hitchhiked to Indiana (without telling his parents) for the first anniversary of Dean's death. After the memorial, Sheridan ended up at the Winslows' farm and met the family. When Ortense learned that Sheridan's parents did not know where he was, she took him inside, had him call home, and made sure he boarded a bus for home the next day.

Sheridan maintained a friendship with the family, never losing his fascination with Dean. It was his dream to create his own personal tribute to the star. "I wanted to focus on the man and his work and the pursuit of his career," he explained.[12] Eventually, Sheridan convinced Warner Bros. that he was the right man to make a new Dean documentary. The world premiere took place at the Cannes Film Festival on May 18, 2005. The next audience to see this tribute was made up of fans attending the 2005 James Dean Fest in Marion, Indiana. The film, a blend of still photographs and television and movie clips, explores Dean's rise from struggling actor to Hollywood star.

Forever Young leaves the audience with a touch of sadness and a sense of triumph. There is little doubt that Dean was destined to be a great actor. He would have enriched the moviegoer's experience in the last fifty years. His performances moved people and touched their lives. He once said that he believed there was "only one true form of greatness for man, if a man can bridge the gap between life and death. . . . [I]f he can live on after he's died, then maybe he was a great man. . . .[13] Based on his own definition, James Byron Dean can claim undying greatness.

Chronology

1930—***July 26***: Winton Dean marries Mildred Wilson in Marion, Indiana.

1931—***February 8***: James Byron Dean is born at home in Marion, Indiana.

1936—The Dean family moves to Santa Monica, California, when Jimmy is five years old.

1940—***July 14***: Mildred Dean dies of cancer at the Dean family home in Santa Monica; ***July 16***: Jimmy returns to Fairmount, Indiana, with Grandmother Emma Dean; ***July 20***: Mildred Dean is buried in Grant Memorial Park in Marion, Indiana. After the funeral, Jimmy stays in Fairmount and makes his home with Marcus and Ortense Winslow, his aunt and uncle.

1943—***November***: Jimmy's cousin, Marcus Dean Winslow, Jr., is born.

1945—Jimmy begins his freshman year at Fairmount High School.

1947—Appears in high-school plays *Mooncalf Mugford* and *Our Hearts Were Young and Gay*.

1948—Appears in play *The Monkey's Paw*; writes "My Case Study"; begins his senior year at Fairmount High; and appears as Frankenstein's monster in *Goon With the Wind*.

1949—Dean turns eighteen. ***April 8***: Takes first place at National Forensic League's contest with his performance of Charles Dickens's *A Madman's Manuscript*. ***April 29***: Performs at the National Forensic Tournament in Longmont, Colorado, and finishes sixth in the semifinals. ***May 16***: Graduates from Fairmount High School. ***May 31***: Leaves Fairmount to live in Los Angeles, California, with his father, Winton Dean, and stepmother, Ethel. ***August 11***: Appears under stage name Byron James in Santa Monica theater production. ***September 12***: Begins classes at Santa Monica College.

1950—Enters UCLA and wins role of Malcolm in university stage production of *Macbeth*.

1951—Drops out of UCLA; appears in Coca-Cola commercial. ***March 25***: Appears in TV drama *Hill Number One*. ***June***: Meets Rogers Brackett while parking cars in lot near CBS. ***July***: Appears in CBS radio program, *Alias Jane Doe*. ***August–October***: Bit parts in *Fixed Bayonets*, *Sailor Beware*, and *Has Anybody Seen My Gal?* ***October 10***: Leaves Los Angeles for New York City.

1952—***February***: Meets Jane Deacy. ***May***: Auditions for Actors Studio with Christine White. Appears in several TV episodes, including "Sleeping Dogs," "Prologue to Glory," and "The Forgotten Children." ***October 9***: Hitchhikes to Fairmount with friends Bast and Sheridan. ***Late October***: Begins rehearsals for *See the Jaguar*. ***December 3***: Debuts on Broadway in play that closes four days later.

1953—Appears in more TV episodes including: "The Hound of Heaven," "The Killing of Jesse James," "Death Is My Neighbor," "Glory in the Flower," "Keep Our Honor Bright," and "A Long Time Till Dawn." November: Auditions for *The Immoralist*. ***December 1***: Screen tests for Warner Bros. film *Battle Cry*.

1954—***February 5***: Meets with director Elia Kazan. ***February 8***: *The Immoralist* opens on Broadway. Dean gives two-weeks notice. ***February 16***: Screen tests for role of Cal in *East of Eden*. ***March 6***: *The New York Times* reports that Dean signed by Kazan for new film. ***April 8***: Flies to Los Angeles with Elia Kazan. ***May 27***: Filming of *East of Eden* begins. ***August 9***: *Eden* filming wraps up. Appears in several TV roles: "Padlocks," "I'm a Fool," and "The Dark, Dark Hour." ***December 6***: First sneak preview of *East of Eden*. ***December:*** Returns to New York City.

1955—***January 4***: Press announces Dean's next film, *Rebel Without a Cause*. Dean returns to Los Angeles later that month. ***February***: Photo shoot with Dennis Stock. ***March 7***: Stock's photo-essay appears in *Life*. ***March 10***: *East of Eden* premieres in New York City. ***March 16***: *Eden* opens in Los Angeles. ***March 26 and 27***: Competes in Palm Springs road races. ***March 30***: Filming begins on *Rebel Without a Cause*. ***May 2***: *Rebel* wraps up. ***May 29***: Competes in Santa Barbara road race. ***June 6***: Joins *Giant* cast in Marfa, Texas. ***July 28***: Films public service announcement with Gig Young. ***September 17***: Dean's last day of work on *Giant*. Dean attends screening of *Rebel Without a Cause*. ***September 22***: Buys Porsche 550 Spyder. ***September 30***: James Dean dies in automobile accident on the way to races in Salinas. ***October 8***: Funeral services held in Fairmount, Indiana. ***October 26***: *Rebel Without a Cause* premieres in New York City.

1956—***October 10***: *Giant* premieres more than a year after Dean's death.

Chapter Notes

Chapter 1. The Big Break

1. Donald Spoto, *Rebel: The Life and Legend of James Dean* (New York: Harper Collins, 1996), p. 157.
2. Ibid.
3. John Howlett, *James Dean: A Biography* (New York: Simon & Schuster, 1975), p. 66.
4. David Loehr, ed., *James Dean: Shooting Star* (London: Bloomsbury Publishing Limited, 1989), p. 63.
5. William Bast, *James Dean: A Biography*, (New York: Ballantine Books, 1956), pp. 102–104.

Chapter 2. James Byron Dean

1. Donald Spoto, *Rebel: The Life and Legend of James Dean* (New York: Harper Collins, 1996), p. 13.
2. Ibid., p. 10.
3. Paul Alexander, *Boulevard of Broken Dreams: The Life, Time, and Legend of James Dean* (New York: Viking, 1994), p. 15.
4. Venable Herndon, *James Dean: A Short Life* (New York: Doubleday & Company, Inc., 1974), p. 22.
5. Wolfgang J. Fuchs, *James Dean: Footsteps of a Giant* (Berlin, Germany: Taco Verlagsgesellschaft unf Agentur mbH, 1989), p. 12.
6. Spoto, p. 14.
7. Ibid., p. 18.
8. Joe Hyams and Jay Hyams, *James Dean: Little Boy Lost* (New York: Warner Books, 1992), p. 9.
9. Joseph Humphreys, *Jimmy Dean on Jimmy Dean* (London: Plexus Publishing, Inc, 1990), p. 8.

10. Ibid.
11. Spoto, p. 23.
12. Ibid, p. 16.
13. Ibid., p. 20.
14. Spoto, p. 22.

Chapter 3. Growing Up in L.A.

1. George Perry, *James Dean* (London: DK, 2005), p. 27.
2. David Loehr, ed., *James Dean: Shooting Star* (London: Bloomsbury Publishing Limited, 1989), p. 18.
3. David Dalton, *James Dean: The Mutant King* (New York: Dell Publishing Co., 1974), p. 14.
4. Donald Spoto, *Rebel: The Life and Legend of James Dean* (New York: Harper Collins, 1996), p. 22.
5. Dalton, p. 14.
6. Spoto, p. 23.
7. Ibid.
8. Ibid.
9. Ibid.
10. Ibid.
11. Ibid.
12. Paul Alexander, *Boulevard of Broken Dreams: The Life, Time, and Legend of James Dean* (New York: Viking, 1994), p. 24.
13. Dalton, p. 16.
14. Spoto, p. 24.
15. Dalton, p. 16.
16. Alexander, p. 24.
17. Loehr, p. 18.
18. Dalton, p. 18.
19. Ibid.

20. Ibid.
21. Spoto, p. 25.
22. Ibid.
23. Dalton, p. 16.

Chapter 4. Orphaned

1. Donald Spoto, *Rebel: The Life and Legend of James Dean* (New York: Harper Collins, 1996), p. 28.
2. Ibid., p. 27.
3. David Dalton, *James Dean: The Mutant King* (New York: Dell Publishing Co., 1974), p. 30.
4. Spoto, p. 30.
5. David Loehr, ed., *James Dean: Shooting Star* (London: Bloomsbury Publishing Limited, 1989), p. 21.
6. Spoto, p. 34; George Perry, *James Dean* (London: DK, 2005), p. 32.
7. David Dalton, *James Dean: American Icon* (New York: St. Martin's Press, 1955), p. 16.
8. Dalton, p. 50.
9. Spoto, p. 30.
10. Dalton, p. 33.
11. Spoto, p. 33.
12. Ibid., p. 37.
13. Ibid., p. 40.
14. Dalton, p. 47.
15. Ibid.
16. Ibid., p. 49.
17. Ibid.
18. Perry, p. 20.
19. Dalton, p. 65.
20. Ibid., p. 64.
21. Loehr, p. 30.

22. Dalton, p. 32.

Chapter 5. Early Acting Jobs

1. David Dalton, *James Dean: The Mutant King* (New York: Dell Publishing Co., 1974), p. 69.
2. John Howlett, *James Dean: A Biography* (New York: Simon & Schuster, 1975), p. 21.
3. George Perry, *James Dean* (London: DK, 2005), p. 60.
4. Ibid.
5. Howlett, p. 23.
6. Dalton, p. 75.
7. Howlett, p. 26.
8. Ibid.
9. Ibid.
10. Venable Herndon, *James Dean: A Short Life* (New York: Doubleday & Company, Inc., 1974), p. 73.
11. David Loehr, ed., *James Dean: Shooting Star* (London: Bloomsbury Publishing Limited, 1989), p. 36.
12. Herndon, p. 81.
13. Dalton, p. 77.
14. Howlett, p. 30.
15. Dalton, p. 78.
16. Loehr, p. 41.
17. Dalton, p. 82.
18. Loehr, p. 42.
19. Perry, pp. 77–78.
20. Howlett, p. 29.
21. Ibid.
22. Ibid., p. 30.
23. William Bast, *James Dean: A Biography* (New York: Ballantine Books, 1956), p. 52.

Chapter 6. The Big City

1. Joseph Humphreys, *Jimmy Dean on Jimmy Dean* (London: Plexus Publishing, Inc, 1990), p. 36.
2. Donald Spoto, *Rebel: The Life and Legend of James Dean* (New York: Harper Collins, 1996), p. 104.
3. Ibid., p. 94.
4. George Perry, *James Dean* (London: DK, 2005), p. 88.
5. Ibid., p. 84.
6. Spoto, p 97.
7. Liz Sheridan, *Dizzy & Jimmy: My Life With James Dean* (Thorndike: G. K. Hall & Co., 2000), pp. 81–82.
8. Ibid., p. 141.
9. Spoto, p. 90.
10. Ibid., p. 102.
11. Perry, p. 85.
12. Spoto, p. 101.
13. Ibid.
14. Perry, p. 88.
15. David Loehr, ed., *James Dean: Shooting Star* (London: Bloomsbury Publishing Limited, 1989), p. 48.
16. John Howlett, *James Dean: A Biography* (New York: Simon & Schuster, 1975), p. 43.
17. Humphreys, pp. 41–42.
18. Perry, p. 90.
19. Spoto, p. 114.
20. William Bast, *James Dean: A Biography* (New York: Ballantine Books, 1956), pp. 84–85.
21. David Dalton, *James Dean: The Mutant King* (New York: Dell Publishing Co., 1974), p. 133.

22. Spoto, p. 118.
23. Ibid., p. 119.

Chapter 7. Discovered

1. John Howlett, *James Dean: A Biography* (New York: Simon & Schuster, 1975), p. 49.
2. David Loehr, ed., *James Dean: Shooting Star* (London: Bloomsbury Publishing Limited, 1989), p. 54.
3. Donald Spoto, *Rebel: The Life and Legend of James Dean* (New York: Harper Collins, 1996), pp. 125–126.
4. Joseph Humphreys, *Jimmy Dean on Jimmy Dean* (London: Plexus Publishing, Inc, 1990), p. 53.
5. Joe Hyams and Jay Hyams, *James Dean: Little Boy Lost* (New York: Warner Books, 1992), p. 82.
6. Ibid.
7. George Perry, *James Dean* (London: DK, 2005), p. 96.
8. Spoto. p. 132.
9. Graham McCann, *Rebel Males: Clift, Brando, and Dean* (New Brunswick: Rutgers University Press, 1993), p. 132.
10. Spoto., p. 134.
11. David Dalton, *James Dean: The Mutant King* (New York: Dell Publishing Co., 1974), p. 166.
12. Humphreys, p. 57.
13. Dalton, p. 154.
14. Perry, p. 100.
15. Loehr, p. 58.
16. Perry, p. 102.
17. Ibid., p. 104.
18. Ibid., p. 109.

Chapter 8. Lights, Camera, Action

1. Donald Spoto, *Rebel: The Life and Legend of James Dean* (New York: Harper Collins, 1996), p. 164.
2. John Howlett, *James Dean: A Biography* (New York: Simon & Schuster, 1975), p. 68.
3. Spoto, p. 164.
4. Ibid.
5. Ibid.
6. David Loehr, ed., *James Dean: Shooting Star* (London: Bloomsbury Publishing Limited, 1989), p. 69.
7. Spoto, p. 164.
8. Venable Herndon, *James Dean: A Short Life* (New York: Doubleday & Company, Inc., 1974), p. 140.
9. David Dalton, *James Dean: American Icon* (New York: St. Martin's Press, 1955), pp. 43–44.
10. Herndon, pp. 144–145.
11. Spoto, p. 162.
12. Ibid.
13. William Bast, *James Dean: A Biography*, (New York: Ballantine Books, 1956), p. 110.
14. Dalton, p. 20.
15. Spoto, p. 168.

Chapter 9. Fame, Fortune, and Romance

1. Joseph Humphreys, *Jimmy Dean on Jimmy Dean* (London: Plexus Publishing, Inc, 1990), p. 77.
2. Ibid.
3. John Parker, *Five for Hollywood* (New York: Carol Publishing Group, 1989), pp. 77–78.
4. Ibid., p. 85.
5. Humphreys, p. 75.
6. Ibid., p. 72.

7. Ibid.
8. David Loehr, ed., *James Dean: Shooting Star* (London: Bloomsbury Publishing Limited, 1989), p. 90.
9. Humphreys, p. 75.
10. Ibid., p. 80.
11. Ibid.
12. Parker, p. 87.
13. Humphreys, p. 84.
14. Ibid.
15. Ibid.
16. Ibid., p. 85.
17. Loehr, p. 94.
18. Ibid., p. 97.
19. George Perry, *James Dean* (London: DK, 2005), pp. 139–141.
20. Humphreys, p. 85.
21. Loehr, p. 105.
22. Perry, p. 129.
23. Loehr, p. 105.
24. Paul Alexander, *Boulevard of Broken Dreams: The Life, Time, and Legend of James Dean* (New York: Viking, 1994), pp. 188–189.
25. Venable Herndon, *James Dean: A Short Life* (New York: Doubleday & Company, Inc., 1974), p. 184.

Chapter 10. Rebel

1. David Dalton, *James Dean: The Mutant King* (New York: Dell Publishing Co., 1974), p. 249.
2. Ibid., p. 250.
3. Ibid., p. 252.
4. George Perry, *James Dean* (London: DK, 2005), p. 149.

5. John Parker, *Five for Hollywood* (New York: Carol Publishing Group, 1989), p. 94.
6. Dalton, p. 253.
7. Ibid., p. 256.
8. Ibid.
9. Joseph Humphreys, *Jimmy Dean on Jimmy Dean* (London: Plexus Publishing, Inc, 1990), p. 92.
10. Ibid., p. 260.
11. Perry, p. 158.
12. Donald Spoto, *Rebel: The Life and Legend of James Dean* (New York: Harper Collins, 1996), pp. 202–203.
13. Ibid., p. 203.
14. Ibid.
15. Paul Alexander, *Boulevard of Broken Dreams: The Life, Time, and Legend of James Dean* (New York: Viking, 1994), p. 204.
16. Dalton, p. 263.
17. Ibid.
18. Ibid.
19. Ibid., p. 257.
20. David Loehr, ed., *James Dean: Shooting Star* (London: Bloomsbury Publishing Limited, 1989), p. 124.
21. Perry, p. 153.
22. Humphreys, p. 97.
23. Ibid.
24. John Howlett, *James Dean: A Biography* (New York: Simon & Schuster, 1975), p. 123.
25. Ibid., p. 121.
26. Dalton, p. 105.

Chapter 11. *Giant*

1. Venable Herndon, *James Dean: A Short Life* (New York: Doubleday & Company, Inc., 1974), p. 193.

2. David Loehr, ed., *James Dean: Shooting Star* (London: Bloomsbury Publishing Limited, 1989), p. 161.
3. Herndon, p. 197.
4. George Perry, *James Dean* (London: DK, 2005), p. 181.
5. Loehr, p. 165.
6. Herndon, p. 216.
7. Ibid.
8. Perry, p. 177.
9. Herndon, p. 217.
10. Perry, p. 182.
11. David Dalton, *James Dean: The Mutant King* (New York: Dell Publishing Co., 1974), pp. 267–268.

Chapter 12. The Last Race

1. Van Holley, *James Dean* (New York: St. Martin's Press, 1995.), p. 277.
2. Ibid.
3. George Perry, *James Dean* (London: DK, 2005), pp. 10–11.
4. David Dalton, *James Dean: The Mutant King* (New York: Dell Publishing Co., 1974), p. 308.
5. Ibid., p. 310.
6. Dalton, p. 281.
7. John Howlett, *James Dean: A Biography* (New York: Simon & Schuster, 1975), p. 158.
8. Perry, p. 199.
9. Pete Hammond, "The Dean Allure," *Cinema's Most Enduring Rebel: Celebrating James Dean's 50th Anniversary* (New York: Variety Custom Publishing, 2005), p. 19.

10. Paul Alexander, *Boulevard of Broken Dreams: The Life, Time, and Legend of James Dean* (New York: Viking, 1994), p. 253.
11. Venable Herndon, *James Dean: A Short Life* (New York: Doubleday & Company, Inc., 1974), p. 236.
12. Ibid., p. 239.
13. Perry, p. 196.
14. Ibid.

Chapter 13. Dean Mania

1. George Perry, *James Dean* (London: DK, 2005), p. 200.
2. Ibid., p. 203.
3. Paul Alexander, *Boulevard of Broken Dreams: The Life, Time, and Legend of James Dean* (New York: Viking, 1994), p. 271.
4. Ibid., p. 273.
5. Ibid., p. 292.
6. Perry, p. 215.
7. Ibid., p. 216.
8. Alexander, p. 294.
9. Perry, p. 215.
10. Ibid.
11. "Dean in His Own Words," *Cinema's Most Enduring Rebel: Celebrating James Dean's 50th Anniversary* (New York: Variety Custom Publishing, 2005), p. 10.
12. "The Documentary: James Dean Forever Young," *Cinema's Most Enduring Rebel: Celebrating James Dean's 50th Anniversary* (New York: Variety Custom Publishing, 2005), p. 4.
13. David Dalton, *James Dean: The Mutant King* (New York: Dell Publishing Co., 1974), p. 378.

Glossary

anemia—A condition in which a person's blood does not have enough red corpuscles and can not carry a normal amount of oxygen.

antisocial—To dislike the company of other people.

articulate—To speak clearly.

automat—Cafeteria where food is served from machines.

beatnik—Name given nonconformists in dress and behavior in the 1950s.

bisexual—Having a sexual orientation to persons of either gender.

blacklist—List of persons that have earned disapproval and are to be boycotted.

blockbuster—Film that sustains widespread popularity and achieves enormous profits.

bungalow—A small one-story house.

charismatic—Magnetic or charming.

conspicuous—Getting attention by behaving in an unusual manner.

eccentric—To behave in a way that is unusual.

eulogy—A formal speech praising a person who has died.

gossip columnist—Someone who writes regular articles for magazines or newspapers filled with rumors about well-known people.

harrow—Farm implement with sharp spikes or disks used to break up soil.

homosexual—Someone who only has intimate relationships with a person of the same gender.

Hoosier—Nickname for a person born in the state of Indiana.

imbibe—To take in or absorb.

immortality—To live forever; to have lasting fame.

improvise—To compose and perform spontaneously.

incestuous—Sexual relations between closely related individuals.

lecherous—Excessive indulgence in sexual activity.

legendary—Having gained herolike fame.

lunatic—Person who is insane.

malaria— Disease spread by mosquito bites. Symptoms are chills and fever.

matador—Bullfighter.

melodrama—A play in which there is exaggeration between the forces of good and evil.

monologue—A play performed by one actor.

nearsighted—When a person can only see things clearly that are close to him or her.

notorious—Well known for negative reasons.

pan—To criticize.

paraplegic—A person who is paralyzed in the lower part of his or her body.

playwright—Someone who writes plays.

profound—Showing great thought.

radium treatments—Chemical treatments used on cancer patients.

shards—Broken pieces of pottery.

soliloquy—Speech in a play where the actor expresses his thoughts aloud.

spontaneous—Taking action with little or no thought.

unconventional—Behaving in an unusual way.

Further Reading

Beath, Warren, and Paul Wheeldon. *James Dean in Death: A Popular Encyclopedia of a Celebrity Phenomenon*. Jefferson, N.C.: McFarland & Co. Publishers, 2005.

Bosworth, Patricia. *Marlon Brando*. New York: Viking Penguin, Inc., 2001.

———. *Montgomery Clift*. Pompton Plains, N.J.: Limelight Editions, 2004.

Cunningham, Terry. *The Timeless James Dean*. Los Angeles: Stagedoor Publishing, 2004.

Finstad, Suzanna. *Natasha: The Biography of Natalie Wood*. New York: Three Rivers Press, 2002.

Jeffers, H. Paul. *Sal Mineo: His Life, Murder & Mystery*. New York: Carroll & Graf Publisher, 2000.

Oleksy, Walter. *James Dean*. San Diego: Lucent Books, 2001.

Perry, George. *James Dean*. New York: DK, 2005.

Stern, Stewart. *Making of Rebel Without a Cause*. Jefferson, N.C.: McFarland & Company, 2004.

Stock, Dennis, and Joe Hyams. *James Dean: Fifty Years Ago*. New York: Harry N. Abrams, 2005.

Internet Addresses

Fairmount Historical Museum
<http://www.jamesdeanartifacts.com>

James Dean Gallery: Museum Exhibit and Archive
<http://www.jamesdeangallery.com>

The Official Site of James Dean
<http://jamesdean.com>

Index